THE HORSEMAN'S NOTEBOOK

THE HORSEMAN'S NOTEBOOK

by
Mary Rose, F.B.H.S.

Foreword by
MICHAEL SIMONS, Esq., M.R.C.V.S.

Illustrations by D. Diane Lent

DAVID McKAY COMPANY, INC.
New York

LIBRARY OF CONGRESS CATALOG CARD NUMBER: 76-53971
ISBN: 0-679-50719-1

10 9 8 7 6 5 4 3 2 1
MANUFACTURED IN THE UNITED STATES OF AMERICA

To My Father
W. Robert Rose

CONTENTS

INTRODUCTION

This book has been written at a time when the horse is increasing in number and popularity on both sides of the Atlantic. In the United Kingdom more than 400,000 horses provide recreation for 1.8 million regular riders: in the United States the number of horses is in excess of 10 million, but I know of no comparable figure for riders. Prosperity has brought riding for recreation within the reach of a large section of the population and they are enjoying it. From riding to horse-owning is a step taken by more and more horsemen and women.

There are two limiting factors to the new popularity of the horse. In the fifty years which have passed since it was the principal means of transport, much of the traditional knowledge of its management has been lost and few people are familiar with its character, temperament and needs. The race of horsemen whose working hours were devoted to their horses and who slept within earshot of their charges is extinct. Every horseman must be his own trainer, stud-groom, strapper and second horseman.

This book deals, systematically and concisely, with the basic knowledge which every owner-rider needs to know. There is usually more than one way of doing a job in stables but the method recommended by the author is always simple, practical and effective.

The Horseman's Notebook makes a notable contribution to the store of horse knowledge and should be on the shelf in every tack-room.

MICHAEL SIMONS

Epsom, Surrey (U.K.)

THE HORSEMAN'S NOTEBOOK

CHAPTER 1

STABLE CONSTRUCTION AND FITTINGS

SITE

Chief Consideration:

1. Dry foundation.   2. Free drainage.   3. Pure air.

4. Good light.   5. Good water supply.

Nature of the Soil

1. Best: Sub-soil of gravel or deep sand. Gives a firm base with free drainage, and dryness.
2. Next best: Any rocky formation—e.g., limestone, chalk or granite.
3. Worst: Stiff clay, deep loam, or peaty and marshy soils. If buildings must be erected on such soils, sub-soil drainage must be extensively adopted.

Foundations

1. Artificial bases, wider than the intended structure, to give stability.
2. If sub-soil water is near the surface, drainage is required.
3. In very damp locations, buildings may have to be raised on arches or piles.
4. Well aerated soil provides ready drainage, and a dry foundation.
5. Sub-soil water near the surface, and no drainage in wet weather, means damp foundation.

Aspect

1. Buildings should be sheltered from most severe prevailing winds.
2. Buildings should not be overshadowed by other structures to the extent of interference with good supply of sunlight and pure air.
3. Buildings are best arranged in echelon or parallel lines.
4. Both above arrangements permit free supply of air and light to each row of stables.
5. Buildings arranged in small enclosures or squares are not good. Permit less free supply of air and give greater chance of contagion when any form of sickness is present.

THE BUILDINGS

Walls

1. Should be at least 12ft. high to the spring of the roof.
2. Should be 1½ to 2 bricks thick and damp-proof.
3. Damp-proofing can be achieved by introducing a 'damp course' of asphalt, or a layer of vitrified brick, into the wall, a little above ground level.
4. Damp-proofing may also be achieved by building double walls with a space in between.
5. The space between double walls is liable to become a refuge for vermin, but does give good protection against dampness from rain beating on exposed brick face. (Brick is very porous.)

Roofs

1. Flat roofs: used only when living rooms or lofts are built overhead. Must be airtight to prevent heated air from stable penetrating rooms above. Offer no natural roof ventilation.
2. Sloping roofs: are best. Their construction secures air space and light, and offers ample natural roof ventilation.

Roofing Materials

1. Tiles: Maintain an equal temperature and afford roof ventilation, but are easily broken or loosened and can leak.
2. Slates: Excellent, but also liable to breakage. Like tiles,
   make good roofs if kept in regular repair, but both
   should have an under-roofing of boards.
3. Stone Flakes: Used in some districts where stone is abundant. Very heavy, clumsy and not recommended.
4. Thatched Roofs and Tarred Felt: Noiseless, warm in cold
   weather and cool in hot weather, but not recommended because of fire risk.
5. Galvanized Iron: Excessively noisy, hot in hot weather and
   cold in cold weather. But cheap and easy to transport,
   is therefore in general use. Should have inner roofing
   of wood.
6. Open Roofs: Roofs without ceilings. May be closed along
   ridge or have louvre board ventilation. Louvres consist of two or more overlapping boards, separated from
   each other by a few inches, and set at such an angle
   that rain and snow cannot beat in.

General Roof Requirements

1. Slope of roof should be at an angle of not more than 45°
   with the horizon.
2. An ideal roof should maintain an equable temperature in
   both hot and cold weather.
3. Roof should be durable.
4. Roof should be noiseless.
5. Roof should be non-flammable.

Floors—Essential Requirements

1. Floors should be laid on solid foundation, and raised above
   outside ground.
2. Non-slippery and impervious to moisture.
3. Smooth, durable and should not strike cold to horse when
   he lies down.
4. Should slope from front to rear of stall or loose box. Slope
   should be only just sufficient to allow drainage.

9

1. A foundation bed of concrete from four to six inches thick must first be laid.
2. Stable bricks, if thoroughly vitrified or the special non-slippery stable variety, make very good flooring.
3. Cobblestones—too uneven. A bad flooring.
4. Stone Slabs—wear smooth and require constant rechipping. Become cracked. Not good flooring.
5. Granite Setts—get very smooth, need rechipping, never give a level standing.
6. Concrete—relatively cheap but not good. If employed, it must be given a rough facing.
7. Asphalt—too easily affected by heat, gets slippery when wet.
8. Wood block and wood plank—too absorbent, slippery when wet.
9. Clay—very good floor, but must be re-laid once a year.
10. "Tartan"—a composition floor that fulfils every requirement. Although obviously the best flooring it is prohibitively expensive.

Dimensions of Loose Boxes and Stalls

1. Loose Boxes for hunters should be 12ft. by 14ft.
2. Loose Boxes for ponies should be 10ft. by 12ft.
3. Stalls should be 5ft. 6in. wide and 11ft. long, from wall to heel post.

VENTILATION

1. Ventilation is of first importance.
2. Air of building must be changed often enough to keep it pure, without allowing draughts to strike the occupants.
3. The body needs a constant and sufficient supply of pure air to enable it to perform hard work and resist the attack of disease.
4. Appearances are not reliable. Unfortunately, horses kept in stuffy, ill-ventilated stables may *look* fatter and more sleek than those occupying cold, fresh stables. However, experience shows that the latter are better able to undertake hard work and resist disease.

5. If stables smell stuffy, the ventilation is defective and the air should be changed more often.
6. In severe climates stables should be closed in winter. Increased air space per head inside the building will allow sufficient pure air for the occupants.

Draught and Chill

1. A draught is a current of air passing through at such a pace that it produces a feeling of cold when it strikes the skin.
2. Effect of draught on warm skin, full of blood, is to drive the blood into the internal organs and produce chill and shivering.
3. The hotter the skin when horse is exposed to a draught, the greater the danger of a chill.
4. Changing stable air too often will cause a constant inrush of cold air and keep horses in a perpetual draught.
5. To avoid having to change air too often, ensure sufficient cubic air space per head. 1,500 to 1,600 cubic feet per head is sufficient stable space overall to achieve this.

Temperature of Stable Air

1. Stables ventilated as directed above, to the extent that temperature inside stable will not differ much from the open air, may be thought to be too cold in winter.
2. Horses do not suffer from cold to the extent man does.
3. Horses stand varying temperatures very well.
4. The only temperature changes really liable to produce sickness are chills from standing in a draught when horse is heated and tired.
5. In cold weather, maintain heat and condition of horse's body by extra food or clothing, not by allowing him to breathe an atmosphere heated by the exclusion of fresh air.

MEANS FOR VENTILATION

1. *Doors*

    (a) Stable doors are not a permanent means of ventilation as they are too often kept shut.
    (b) Where loose boxes have direct access to a yard by individual stable doors; door should be in two parts. The upper portion can then be hooked back and left open.

11

2. *Windows*

(a) Main inlet for fresh air.

(b) Should be arranged along both outer walls of stable, one over each stall or loose box.

(c) Should be hinged from lower edge, or from centre, so they may be opened with an inward slant.

(d) Should be protected with iron bars.

(e) With windows on each side of the stable, those on the leeward side should always be open. In calm weather, those on both sides should be open.

(f) Amount of inlet space required per horse is not less than one square foot.

(g) Loose boxes should always face south, if possible. Window should be on same side as the door.

3. *Louvre Boards*

(a) Fitted under the ridge of roof they act as outlets for heated, foul air.

(b) Should be sufficiently broad and overlapping, and set at an angle acute enough to prevent rain beating in.

(c) Should be permanently fixed open. If movable, they will always be shut.

4. *Ventilating Cowls and Tubes*

(a) Foul air can be extracted by means of cowls and tubes constructed so that the wind passes over an upward slant, or through a narrow slit, and creates a continual vacuum below, thus drawing up the foul air.

(b) Any patterns which permit birds to nest in them are useless.

(c) Cowls and Tubes must be of a pattern which allows them to act equally well from whatever direction the wind blows.

Direction of Air

1. Direction taken by current of air entering a stable is determined by the slant of the inlet through which it comes.

2. With windows sloping upwards, the air will be thrown up and well over the animals underneath.

12

3. Air is cooler as it comes in, and therefore heavier than the air inside the stable.
4. The cooler air will therefore descend and be spread among the animals on the opposite side.
5. Air is therefore well diffused and slightly warmed before reaching horses and risk of draught is avoided.

DRAINAGE

Requirements for efficient stable drainage

1. A floor level from side to side, but sloping sufficiently from front to rear to allow drainage to back of stall.
2. An exit hole, which should be draught proof, connecting with an open gulley outside.
3. A shallow, open, surface drain behind the walls to convey collected fluid to the outside drain or sewer.
4. Standing should be as level as possible, the slope the minimum necessary for drainage.
5. Drain should be shallow. In a long stable, drain should slope from the centre towards both sides.
6. Closed or underground drains, because they are hidden from view, may be difficult to keep clean, or may be forgotten.
7. All drains should be free of sharp angles. A 'trap' should be provided, where stable drainage runs into the outside drain or sewer, to prevent the return of sewer gas.

STABLE DOORS

1. Doors should be 8ft. high and 4ft. wide. Should be hinged or hung on rollers.
2. Half-doors, top and bottom portions opening separately, are excellent. Top half can usually be left open for ventilation. Lower half must be high enough to prevent horse from jumping over.

3. Horses like to look out. Therefore 'grilles' are sometimes provided for fastening across the open top half of the door. This prevents biting at passers-by, loosening the top bolt, and checks weaving.
4. Traversing doors should be hung on rollers from above and fitted with large, smooth handles which could not injure a loose horse.

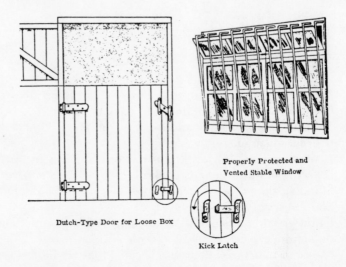

Dutch-Type Door for Loose Box

Properly Protected and
Vented Stable Window

Kick Latch

5. All doors giving access direct to a loose box should open outwards. If an animal becomes cast in his box near the door, it is then possible to open the door.

LATCHES

1. Should be strong, and easily turned.
2. Should have large, flush handles, which offer no projections to injure loose horses..
3. Latches of loose box doors of the half-door type should be designed so that horse cannot open them.
4. On loose box doors of that type, two latches are necessary, one at the top and one at the bottom. The bottom latch can be a foot operated latch, to save constant bending.

WINDOWS

1. Should be hinged along lower border, or in the centre, so that they open with an inward slant.
2. If possible, each horse should have a window over his stall. Sufficient light in a stable is very important.
3. The lower edge of the window should be 8ft. from the floor.
4. Windows should be fastened by some means which leaves no rope or projection for the horse to play with, or in which to become entangled.
5. Windows should be protected by iron bars on the inside.
6. Sash windows are unsuitable for a stable.

STALLS

PARTITIONS AND BAILS

1. Partition in front of horses should prevent them seeing or touching each other.
2. Side partitions should also prevent horses seeing or touching each other at the front, and should be high enough to prevent all chance of a horse kicking over the top, at the back of the stall.
3. 'Bails' are frequently used for the separation of stalls.
4. 'Bails' may range from a simple wood or iron pole, to a deep, heavy boarding.
5. The 'bail' is either supported by attachment to the manger in front and the stall post, behind; or hung from the roof.
6. 'Bails' should be approximately the length of the stall.
7. They should be hung sufficiently high to prevent a horse getting a leg over.
8. If suspended from the roof, stout cord with quick release knot should be used. Chains and wires should not be used.
9. Hang bails slightly higher at the front end than at the back.
10. Disadvantages of bails over kicking boards—no protection against bullying or kickers.

15

KICKING BOARDS

1. Preferably double depth of boarding, but may be only single depth, as an addition to ordinary bail.
2. May be easily attached or removed when necessary.
3. Boards should be strongest possible. Wood with very strong grain.
4. Horses kick very hard and if wood gives way the offender is not only encouraged, but may also be seriously injured. If horse gets leg through the gap made by kicking he may injure another animal.

STABLE FITTINGS

1. The fewer the better.
2. A ring at breast-level, for tying horse up to.
3. Other rings at eye-level, for short-racking and for hay net.
4. All rings must be very firmly fitted.

Mangers

1. Should be 3ft. 6in. from the ground.
2. Should be large, broad and have completely smooth surface and all corners well rounded.
3. Broad shallow manger is preferable to a deep, narrow one. A greedy horse cannot plunge his mouth deeply into the food and seize large mouthfuls.
4. Rim should be broad enough to prevent horse being able to seize it in his teeth and thus encourage crib biting.

Hay racks

1. Hay racks fitted above head level not good. They oblige the horse to feed at an unnatural level and there is a risk of getting dust and hay seeds in horse's eyes.
2. A deep hay manger at the same level as the manger, which can only be entered from the top, is the most economical kind of hay rack. This hay manger should be narrower at the base than at the top, reducing risk of horse banging his knees.

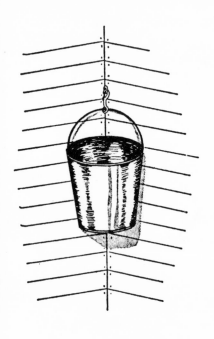

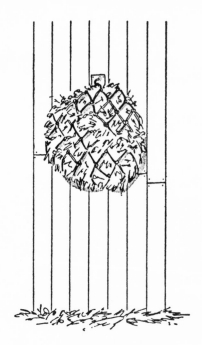

Properly Hung Bucket   Correctly Tied

3. Hay may be fed from the ground. Natural position for horse but method is wasteful. Much hay gets trampled and soiled.

4. Haynets are most efficient and economical method of feeding hay. Also permit accurate weighing of hay fed.

Water Supply

1. Automatic water bowls are efficient and labour-saving. Best type has closed compartment with ball-cock works.

2. Do not site automatic water bowls near manger or hay rack—they may become blocked with food.

3. If water is supplied in a bucket, a large, hinged ring, about 3ft. from ground, preferably in the corner, may be used. The bucket is attached to it with a spring clip. This prevents the bucket being knocked over.

General

1. All fittings, e.g., latches, window fastenings, etc., in a stable must be flush with walls or woodwork, or at least, must not offer any projections on which a horse could tear himself.

2. For the same reason, no nails should be driven into the walls.

3. Electric light switches should be placed outside the loose boxes, in a position where horse cannot interfere with them.

4. All light switches should be of a special "stable" type, designed to prevent electrocution should a shod horse seize them with his teeth.

BIBLIOGRAPHY

Peter C. Smith (ARIBA), *The Design and Construction of Stables*.

Henry Wynmalen, *Horse Breeding and Stud Management*, chapters 2 and 3.

The British Horse Society, *The Manual of Horsemanship*, pp. 130-139.

CHAPTER 2

DAILY ROUTINE

HORSES are creatures of habit and thrive best if cared for according to a fairly strict routine. Specimen programme as a guide to the daily routine is set out below—adjustments will, of course, be necessary to meet varying conditions:

6.30 a.m.   Morning Stables.
Look round horse to ensure he has suffered no injury during the night. Horse should look towards you as he hears you enter stable—if he shows no interest, something may be wrong. Check that he has eaten up his night feed and hay. Check that there are the usual amount of normal-looking droppings in box.
Put on headcollar, adjust rugs, water.
Feed small quantity of hay to keep horse occupied, and if necessary, tie him up.
Muck out.
Pick out feet into muck skip.
Throw up rugs and quarter (i.e., brush off stable stains and surface dirt, sponge eyes, nose and dock, brush out mane and tail).
Replace rugs.

7.30 a.m.   First feed.

9.00 a.m.   Remove droppings.
Remove rugs and saddle up.
Exercise.
On return, remove bridle and saddle and allow horse to stale and drink before putting on headcollar and tying him up to groom.

11.30 a.m. Groom.
Put on day rugs.
Refill water bucket.
Second feed.
Feed full net of hay.
Set fair stable and yard.

4.00 p.m.	Tie horse up.
	Remove droppings.
	Pick out feet.
	Shake up bedding.
	Remove day rug and rug up with night rug.
	Fill water bucket.
4.30 p.m.	Remove headcollar.
	Third feed.
	Clean saddlery.
7.00 p.m.	Remove droppings and shake up bedding.
	Refill water bucket.
	Feed full net—or final ration—of hay.
	Fourth feed.

STABLE TOOLS

Tools required for mucking out horse bedded on:

Straw—5-prong fork or pitch fork, stable broom, shovel, wheelbarrow.

Shavings—10-prong fork, shovel, broom, grass rake, wheelbarrow.

Sawdust—Ditto—(wire potato basket may also be used).

Peat Moss—Same as sawdust.

Also required under all systems—dung skip—preferably the rubber or plastic variety, to avoid possibility of injury.

MUCKING OUT

Straw

Consists of removing soiled portions of bedding and droppings, sweeping floor, and relaying day-bed or bedding down.

Art of good mucking out lies in shaking straw. Start at door and throw clean straw to back, or to one side of box. Shaking causes heavier, soiled straw to fall through prongs of fork and ensures maximum saving of straw. Wet straw will dry in sunshine and is then re-usable, so, if possible, remove it and spread it out to dry. Floor must be thoroughly swept all over at least every two days and allowed to dry out. Therefore, throw clean straw up to right wall one day and left wall the next.

Clay floors particularly develop wet patches—sprinkle with lime every two or three days to keep sweet.

Replace bedding, shaking well so that straws lie evenly over floor. Test depth with fork—should not strike through to floor.

Shavings

Remove droppings and very wet patches with fork. Rake dry shavings from sides of box to centre to give even depth over floor.

Sawdust

Treat as shavings. Or—rake top two inches of bed into pile, shovel into potato basket and shake sawdust through. Deposit wet sawdust and droppings left in basket into barrow. Repeat until all soiled bedding is removed. Rake surface, but don't dig deep.

Peat Moss

Treat as sawdust.

After mucking out, wash out water bucket, refill and replace in box.

MANURE PIT

If limited in size and close to stables, must be emptied frequently.

If manure is to be stacked and rotted, choose site well away from stables. Make three heaps—(1) the oldest, well-rotted manure ready for garden use; (2) discontinued pile in process of rotting; (3) pile in process of formation.

Muck heaps should be close packed (trample, or beat down with shovel) and well squared off—assists decomposition and heat generated inhibits fly breeding.

Shavings, sawdust and peat moss are sometimes difficult to dispose of, so ample space is needed well away from stable.

SECURING HORSES

Horses are secured in stables by headcollar and rope attached to back "D" of noseband. Tie either to manger ring, or pass rope through ring and secure to "log". Log is placed at the end of the rope, so preventing horse getting leg over rope—essential in tie stall.

To "short-rack"—tie up to ring on wall at eye level. Use some recognised form of quick-release knot.

To place horse on pillar reins—turn him round in tie-stall and fasten the reins or chains which hang on heel posts to the side "D's" of headstall.

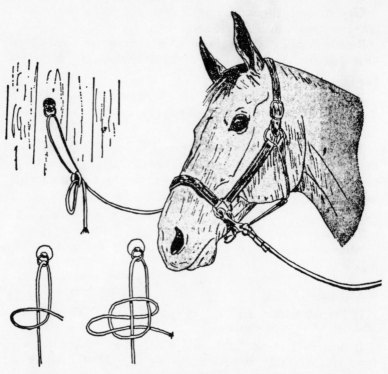

Correct method of securing horse, showing non-slip, quick-release knot.

PADDOCKING

Turning horse out in paddock either for exercise or grass. Lead horse to paddock—use long leadrope and both hands. Don't try to outpull a horse, he will usually respond to a quick snap on the rope. Never wrap leadrope or reins around hand or wrist. Lead horse through gate and turn him round to face gate. Close gate and then remove leadrope quietly. If paddocking for exercise in small enclosed space, remain in centre and "loose school" horse for five or ten minutes—many horses simply stand still when turned out alone. In cold weather, paddock in New Zealand rug. Lungeing is often used in place of loose schooling. In this case the horse is lunged, either from a head collar or lungeing cavesson, at walk and trot, simply for exercise. Lungeing prevents the possibility of the horse rolling in the mud.

EXERCISE AND WORK

Difference—exercise is the procedure of giving a horse sufficient activity to keep him healthy and fit without causing undue exertion or loss of condition. Generally, prolonged periods at steady jog on sound, safe going, conducted by groom. Work denotes owner riding for pleasure and includes canters, gallops, school work, jumping, hunting and showing, all of which may be expected to cause some effort.

Exercise and work must be co-ordinated to produce a fit, trained horse. To exercise during periods of heavy frost, snow or ice—lay down circular straw track (good use for muck heap).

EVENING STABLES

Remove droppings, using muck skip, and pick out feet—into skip. Shake up bed if kept bedded down all day, or lay bed, shaking out straw. If shavings or sawdust are being used, add new bedding as required. Wash out and refill water bucket. Feed: If feeding four times, give bulk of hay after fourth feed. Alternatively, give bulk of hay at 5 or 6 p.m. and return about 8–9.30 p.m., water and give late feed.

Late Watering—filling water bucket late in evening—desirable. Ensures horse has water during the night. (He will drink after eating hay so bucket must in any case be refilled after final feeding.) Late watering gives opportunity to check that all is well for the night.

GENERAL RULES

Stick to fixed daily routine whenever possible.
Exercise is only exception—vary route.
Check horse frequently during day, but allow ample opportunity for real rest and quiet.
Train yourself to "observe".
Speak before entering box or touching horse.
Move quietly. Anticipate reactions of horse. THINK.

BIBLIOGRAPHY

Manual of Horsemanship, pp. 139-141 and 212.
Top Form Book of Horse Care, pp. 74, 79-80, 30-31.

CHAPTER 3

BEDDING

BEDDING is necessary for the following reasons.

1. To prevent injury and encourage horse to lie down in comfort.
2. To prevent draughts and to provide warmth around the lower legs.
3. To encourage horse to stale, and to prevent jar to feet.
4. As an absorbent or drainage material.
5. As a means of assisting in keeping horse clean and air pure.

TYPES OF BEDDING

Bedding may be divided into two categories:
1. Absorbent—preferable where there is no stable drainage.
2. Drainage—used where there is adequate drainage.

Absorbent Bedding
Peat Moss
Tan
Sawdust
Drainage Bedding
Straw
Other forms of litter, e.g., ferns, etc.
Wood shaving occupy an intermediate position.

DEGREE OF ABSORPTIVE POWERS

Forms of bedding listed in order, low to high.
1. Sand (only absorbs quarter its weight in water).
2. Wheat straw.
3. Oat straw.
4. Barley straw.
5. Peat Moss (absorbs 6-10 times its weight in water).
6. Wood shaving.
7. Sawdust.
8. Tan.

PROPERTIES OF GOOD BEDDING

To fulfil necessary requirements of health, comfort, cleanliness and economy, bedding should be:
1. Dry.
2. Soft.
3. Absorbent of fluids and gases.
4. Clean in use.
5. Easily obtainable.
6. In good condition.
7. Good conductor of heat.
8. Not injurious if eaten.
9. Light in colour for good appearance.
10. Readily disposable.

EFFECTS OF BEDDING ON HORSES' FEET

1. Sawdust, tan bark, and peat moss are bad conductors of heat. These materials can become overheated, soggy and harmful to horses' feet if not properly managed. If the bed is not kept clean and dry, horse may get thrush, leading to canker and contracted heels.

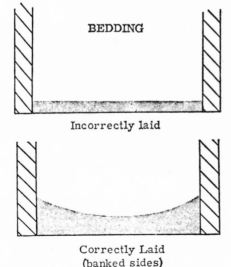

Incorrectly laid

Correctly Laid
(banked sides)

25

However, these types of bedding are good, clean, bright, comfortable and cheap. In clean conditions, horses' feet will suffer no injurious effects.

2. Straw is a good conductor of heat and straw bedding keeps horses' feet cooler and has no injurious effect on them.

STRAW VERSUS OTHER BEDDING MATERIALS

Straw—Old straw better than new—dryer, more elastic (provided it has been well stored). Whatever type is used should be of good quality—if straw undergoes too much bruising and breaking it loses elasticity and durability. Short straw is more economical than long, but harder to work with.

Wheat Straw—generally considered the best, light, durable and not usually eaten.

Oat Straw—sometimes cheaper but less durable. Makes good bedding—disadvantage is that horses often eat it (oat straw has low feeding value).

Barley Straw—cheapest but inferior in appearance and durability. Beards or "awns" cause itching and skin irritations, and can cause stamping, kicking and rubbing. Barley straw can cause colic if eaten. However, barley straw from a combine harvester is often free of "awns" and makes fairly good bedding.

Sawdust—cheap and economical in many areas. Should be dry and well seasoned; pine sawdust has a deodorising effect and properties. May block drains unless precautions are taken in advance. Is easy to keep clean and light to work but hasn't the pleasing appearance of straw.

Wood Shavings—Notes under Sawdust also apply to shavings, but shavings are less dusty. Now available in convenient bales in some areas, which makes handling easier. Good bedding. Both shavings and sawdust require constant attention and frequent removal of droppings. Horses do not eat bed and therefore they are useful for horses with heaves, etc. May also be used very satisfactorily together, when sawdust forms the under layer.

Peat Moss—Comments under Sawdust and Wood Shavings apply also to peat moss, but it is heavier to work, darker in appearance, and requires just as much attention as sawdust. However, peat makes an excellent bed, when wet, soiled patches are removed frequently and bed forked and raked daily, and is particularly valuable where risk of fire is a consideration. May be dusty when first put down. Disposal sometimes difficult.

Sand—good bedding in hot, dry climates—gets too cold where there is dampness. A horse can get serious colic from eating sand. Never use ocean beach sand, which horses may lick for the sake of the salt.

Combination, Continental or Deep Litter System—Peat moss (or sometimes sawdust) to a depth of six inches may be used as a base with generous bed of straw on top. Droppings are removed frequently but no "mucking out" is done, instead fresh straw is sprinkled on top of the old bed. Foundation of peat is not necessary and bed can be made entirely of straw.

Advantages—warm, horses lie down frequently. Labour saving, very easy to manage.
Disadvantages—if sawdust is used as a base, may become heated and maggoty. Needs removing completely once or twice a year and for this a tractor and fork lift are desirable. Horses' feet need very close attention to avoid thrush.

Other Bedding Materials—corncobs, peanut hulls, oat hulls, bracken and pine needles.
Whatever bedding is used it is essential to keep it clean, remove droppings and soiled portions frequently and replace the soiled bedding with a fresh, clean supply.

BIBLIOGRAPHY

Manual of Horsemanship, pp. 139-141.

First Aid Hints for the Horse Owner, Lt.-Col. W. E. Lyon, pp. 32-34.

Top Form Book of Horse Care, Frederick Harper, pp. 73-74.

CHAPTER 4

GROOMING

GROOMING is the daily attention necessary to the feet and coat of the stabled horse.

OBJECTIVES OF GROOMING

The skin is a vital organ and grooming is as essential to a horse's good health as it is to his appearance. Stabled horses are denied the opportunity to live a natural life, to roll and to exercise at will, the skin and the feet suffer unless properly cared for.

1. To promote health — grooming removes waste products, stimulates the circulation of blood and lymph and improves muscle tone.
2. To maintain condition.
3. To prevent disease.
4. To ensure cleanliness.
6. To improve appearance.

Grooming also helps considerably with the 'gentling' of a young horse.

GROOMING TOOLS

Hoof Pick: for cleaning out the feet.

Dandy Brush: for removing heavy dirt, caked mud and dust. Of special value for care of grass-kept horse. Use very sparingly and gently on Thoroughbreds or horses recently clipped. Do not use on head, mane or tail.

Body Brush: for removal of dust, scurf and grease from the coat, mane and tail.

Curry Comb: Metal or rubber—for cleaning the body brush. The rubber variety may be used on horses with heavy coats to help remove caked mud and dirt, particularly in spring when horse is changing his coat. Use gently in small circle, never curry bony parts, i.e., head or lower legs.

Water Brush: for use, damp, on the mane, tail and feet.

Sponge: for cleaning eyes, nose and dock. Two advisable.

Wisp: for promoting circulation and for massage.

Mane and Tail Comb: usually of metal—may be used to help comb out tangled manes and tails of grass-kept ponies, but generally used to assist in pulling mane or tail.

Stable Rubber: for a final polish after grooming.

Sweat Scraper: long, flexible blade of smooth metal—used to remove excess sweat or water.

Electric or hand clippers: and/or scissors, are used for 'trimming' (see section 'Clipping and Trimming').

Body Brush

Curry Comb

Water Brush

Tail Comb

Wisp

Sponge

Dandy Brush

Hoof Pick

Stable Rubber

1. Assemble articles listed above—these should be kept togethei in a grooming box or wire basket. A bucket of water will also be required.

2. Put headstall on horse, who must be cool and dry, and remove rugs (if being worn). In stable, short rack horse, if grooming outside (which is often more pleasant in summer) tie horse up short to a secure ring in a wall or a tree.

3. Pick out feet with hoof pick. Pick up each foot in turn, remove whatever may be lodged in foot with point of pick, working always from heel towards the toe. In this way there is no risk of the pick penetrating the soft parts of the frog. Clear the cleft of frog and look for any signs of thrush. Tap shoe to see that it is secure, and run tips of fingers around clenches to ensure that none have risen.

   It is permissible, when picking out the feet, to lift the off feet from the near side.

   It is correct, when picking out feet, to place a dung skip

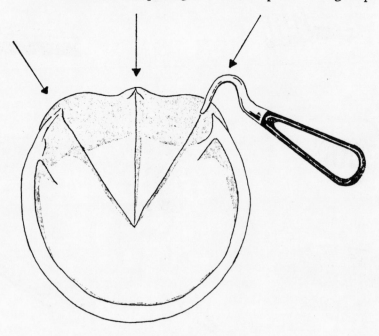

How to Pick Out a Hoof

near enough to allow dirt to fall directly into it. If this is not done, it is necessary to sweep up after picking out feet.

4. Using the Dandy Brush or Rubber Curry Comb, remove all caked dirt, sweat marks, etc., from horse's body. Begin at the poll on the near side and work gradually all over the body paying particular attention to the saddle and girth region, belly, points of the hocks, fetlocks and pasterns.

The dandy brush may be held in either hand and is used with a to-and-fro motion. Avoid using this brush on tender parts of the body. When working on the hind limbs, grasp the tail with the free hand—this not only prevents the horse swishing his tail in your face, but also discourages a ticklish horse from kicking. Never stand directly behind the horse but keep slightly to one side or the other. Never sit or kneel beside the horse to brush his lower legs, always bend or squat.

5. With the Body Brush, which has short, close-set hairs designed to reach right through the coat to the skin beneath, start grooming in the poll region on the near side. With the Body Brush in the left hand and the Curry Comb in the right, start working on the near side. Stand well back, work with a slightly bent arm and supple wrist and lean the weight of the body behind the brush.

The brush is used in short circular strokes in the direction of the lay of the coat, never to-and-fro. After every four or five strokes, clean the brush by drawing it smartly across the teeth of the curry comb, and tap the dirt from the comb out on the floor.

When the near side is completed, go to the off side and change hands. Before grooming the off side, throw the mane across to the wrong side of the neck and brush the crest thoroughly. Continue grooming the off side of the horse and, having finished, groom the mane. Begin at the withers. Insert a finger of the free hand into the mane to separate a few locks of hair and brush the ends of these first to remove tangles. Then brush the roots. Work slowly up the neck, dealing with a few locks of hair at a time.

To do the head, ensure that the horse is turned away from the manger, drop the headstall and fasten it temporarily around the neck. Dispense with the curry comb and use the free hand to steady the horse's head. Work quietly to avoid injury to the tender parts and bony projections. On completion of the head, replace the headstall. Finally, brush the tail. Here again, deal with a few locks of hair at a time and start at the bottom of the tail and work up towards the roots to remove tangles gently and avoid pulling out hairs.

Do not use the Dandy Brush on the mane or tail as it removes and breaks the hairs.

6. Take the wisp, damp it slightly and use it vigorously by bringing it down with a bang in the direction of the lay of the coat. Wisping is a form of massage to develop and harden muscles, to produce a shine on the coat by drawing oil from the glands in the skin, and to stimulate the skin by improving the blood supply. Give special attention to those parts where the muscles are hard and flat, i.e., sides of neck, quarters and thighs. Avoid all bony prominences and the tender loin region.

7. Wring out the sponge in the bucket of warm water so that it is left soft, clean and damp. Sponge the eyes first, work away from the corners and then around the eyelids. Wring out the sponge again and sponge the muzzle region, including lips and inside and outside of nostrils, in that order. Wring out the sponge again and sponge the dock region. Lift the tail as high as possible and sponge the whole dock region, including the skin of the under surface of the tail. Sponging refreshes a stabled horse and is appreciated greatly.

8. 'Lay' the mane—dip the end hairs of the water brush in the bucket of water and apply flat to the mane working from the roots downwards. Mane is left slightly damp and in the desired position.

9. Wash the feet, using one end of the water brush. Keep the thumb of the hand holding the foot pressed well into the hollow of the heel to prevent water becoming lodged there. Washing the feet is best omitted in cold weather.

10. When hoof is dry, using a small brush dipped in hoof oil, coat the entire hoof with the oil, starting with the sole and frog, including the bulbs of heels and the wall as far up as the coronet. This not only improves appearance but is good for brittle or broken feet.

32

11. Go all over the horse with the stable rubber to remove the last traces of dust from the coat. Fold the rubber into a flat bundle, damp it and wipe the coat in the direction of the lay of the hair.

12. Replace rugs and put on tail bandage—if tail is pulled.

An experienced groom will spend from ½ to ¾ of an hour with each horse. A novice will need longer. Thoroughness brings its own reward—a well groomed horse is not only a pleasing sight but a healthy animal.

GROOMING MACHINES

Many excellent models are on the market. Used intelligently they are a great boon in large stables. The correct method of use is to machine groom every second or third day and to wisp on intervening days.

HOW TO MAKE A WISP

Using soft hay and a bucket of water, make a tightly woven rope about 6 to 8 feet long by wetting the hay and twisting it round and round. Fashion two loops at one end of the rope, one slightly longer than the other. Twist each loop in turn beneath the remainder of the rope until all is used up. The end of the rope is then twisted through the bottom of each loop and tucked beneath the last twist. A properly made wisp should be hard and firm and no larger than can conveniently be grasped in the hand.

BATHING THE HORSE

Racehorses commonly get a washing when lathered up after a race, but a bath is not a short cut to good grooming. Never wash a horse unless he can be thoroughly dried, as he is susceptible to chills. In hot, dry weather, if the horse is sweaty after work, he will appreciate a bath. Ensure that he has been walked sufficiently to be cool, if not dry, before bathing. Never stand a horse still while blowing hard and bath him. Use warm water and a wash mixture or mild soap. Use plenty of water and rinse thoroughly. Remove surplus water with sweatscraper and sponge up the remaining water with a clean, damp sponge. Finally, rub horse as dry as possible, paying particular attention to the legs and heels, and walk him dry in the sunshine. When dry, brush all over with Body Brush.

WHEN TO GROOM

1. *Quartering.* Done first thing in the morning.
   Pick out feet. Sponge eyes, nose and dock. Throw up rugs and quickly brush exposed parts of body. Pay particular attention to removal of stains on flanks, using sponge and water if necessary. Object is to make horse look tidy for morning exercise. Note, quartering is carried out without undoing or removing the roller or surcingle.

2. *Strapping.* Is the thorough grooming of the animal outlined above. Preferably done on return from exercise when the skin is warm, pores open and dust and scurf rise easily to the surface. If, however, horse is fed on return from exercise, allow him time to take feed undisturbed.

3. *Brush-over or Set-fair.* Done in the evening when rugs are changed and box set-fair.
   Pick out feet. Brush over lightly and wisp, if time permits.

THE GRASS-KEPT HORSE

Some modification of grooming procedure is necessary when horse is kept at grass.

The body brush—which cannot be used efficiently on an animal that rolls every day or on one with a long winter coat—is designed to remove grease and dandruff from the coat of the horse. The horse kept outside needs this grease to keep his body warm and to waterproof his hair. In any case, the skin of a horse living a natural life will be in a healthy condition.

Grooming should be limited to attention to the feet, a good brush down with Dandy Brush or Rubber Curry Comb to remove mud, attention to mane and tail with the body brush, and sponging of eyes, nose and dock.

BIBLIOGRAPHY

The Manual of Horsemanship, pp. 160-168.

Top Form Book of Horse Care, pp. 75-78.

First Aids Hints for the Horse Owner, Lt.-Col. W. E. Lyon, pp. 19-21.

CHAPTER 5

WATERING AND FEEDING

HORSES require Water and Food. Of the two, water is the most essential. Horses can survive some time without food, but cannot live long without water.

WATERING

Uses of water

1. Largest constituent of the body. Foal's body consists of 80 per cent water and adult horse 50 per cent.
2. Nutrition is performed by fluids. Without water, blood circulation is impaired and digestive processes impossible.
3. Lime in the water assists in the formation of bone and other tissue.
4. Water necessary to quench thirst and keep temperature down.
5. Water aids excretion.

Quantity

1. A horse drinks between six and ten gallons a day.
2. A horse makes six gallons of saliva for mastication every twenty-four hours.
3. A fresh supply of clean water should be constantly available.

Purity

Water given to horses should be fresh, clean and untainted. Running water—i.e., a stream—is best. Moderately hard water contains carbonates of lime and magnesium in addition to traces of common salt. It is more refreshing than soft water. Water that is too hard can produce adverse effects on skin and coat— harsh coat results but disappears if soft water is used.

RULES OF WATERING

1. Constant supply of fresh clean water should be always available.
2. If this is not possible, water at least three times a day in winter and six times a day in summer. Water before feeding.
3. If water is not constantly available to horse, allow half to one hour after feeding before watering.
4. Do not warm water artificially, unless the horse is brought in hot (which should not happen) and then only warm to 80 degrees Fahrenheit.
5. If a bucket of water is left constantly with the horse, change it and swill out bucket at least twice a day, and refill as necessary (probably four or five times a day). Standing water absorbs ammonia and other impurities from the air and becomes flat.
6. Horses that have been deprived of water should not be given as much as they can drink. Give small quantities frequently until system is back to normal.
7. Remove water and do not allow horse to drink for three or four hours before racing or any fast work. A full stomach presses on the diaphragm and this restricts breathing.
8. During continuous work water every two hours. Do not allow horse to drink while actually hunting, however, but let him drink a small quantity on the way home.

METHODS OF WATERING

Stabled horses

1. Trough in Stable Yard. Useful for offering a drink to horses returning from work before putting them into the stable. Unsatisfactory as the only means of watering stabled horses as it necessitates taking horse out of the stable to the trough several times a day.
2. Water Bowl in Manger. If bowl is kept clean and full this is satisfactory. Bowl in Manger is likely to get dirty and clogged with food.
3. Automatic Drinking Bowls. Satisfactory if kept clean and tested each day. Should be sited away from manger and hay rack. The main disadvantages are that shallowness prevents horse taking full drink, and groom cannot tell if horse is drinking properly (sometimes an early indication of sickness).

4. Bucket in corner of box. Perhaps the most satisfactory system. Bucket may either be placed on the floor or suspended from special ring at breast height. Bucket should be placed, ideally, in corner away from manger and away from the door, but within sight of the door. Buckets must be emptied and swilled out and refilled at least twice each day, and topped up three or four times.

Horses at grass

5. Rivers and Streams. Good system of watering horses at grass provided the river or stream is running water with a gravel bottom and good approach. Shallow water and a sandy bottom may result in small quantities of sand being taken into stomach with the water, which will lead eventually to sand colic.

6. Ponds. If stagnant, unsuitable. Other watering arrangements necessary in addition.

7. Field Troughs. If filled from a piped water supply troughs provide the best method of watering horses at grass. Troughs should be from three to six feet in length and about eighteen inches deep. They must have an outlet in the bottom for emptying so that they can be easily cleaned. Place trough on well drained land, clear of trees, so that surrounds do not become too muddy and trough is not clogged with leaves. Troughs require attention twice a day during frost and snow. Troughs should be free of sharp edges or projections on which a horse might be injured. If filled by means of a tap, it should be placed at ground level and the pipe from tap to trough fitted close to the side and edge of the trough. A projecting tap near the trough is dangerous to horses. Best means of keeping trough full is an enclosed compartment at one end containing a ball-cock apparatus.

FEEDING

Objectives of feeding

1. To provide material for repair of body wastes and to put flesh on the horse.
2. For development.
3. To supply energy for work.

Groups of food

1. Proteins—vital for the maintenance and growth of animal tissues.

2. Carbohydrates, or starch, oil or fat, and sugar, are energy and heat producing substances. Cannot replace proteins or fulfil their functions.

3. Fibre. Woody substance with little feeding value. Necessary to the horse whose system requires bulk. Fibre stimulates digestive processes and aids in assimilation of digestible matter.

4. Minerals. Salt, lime, magnesium, potash and iron. Horses need these minerals and mineral deficiency is liable to affect health adversely. Horses like salt and rarely get enough. It is good practice to provide lumps of rock-salt in all fields, and mineral salt licks in each loose box.

5. Vitamins. Important elements vital to health and present in fresh-grown foods—e.g., grasses, fruit, roots, stalks and leaf of maize. Carotene, the matter responsible for colouring these foods and for the blue-green colour of good hay, is convertible into vitamin A. Carotene is present only in infinitesimal traces but is very important.

Digestion

Starts in the mouth and continues throughout the body until the. waste portion of the food leaves the body in the form of dung.

Mastication

1. Becomes less good with age, because teeth become irregular.
2. The sweet smell of food and the motion of the jaws encourages saliva, which plays a vital role in mastication.
3. Horses should be encouraged to eat slowly. To do this, chaff (chopped hay) may be added to the feed. Causes horse to chew rather than bolt food.

Rules of good feeding.

1. Keep mangers scrupulously clean. Allow no traces of the previous feed to remain.
2. Feed little and often. Horse has small stomach for his size and the natural way for him to live is with the stomach nearly always two-thirds full.
3. Feed plenty of bulk. Horse has small stomach but large capacity intestine. Hay and grass are main bulk feeds. Adequate bulk is essential for a successful digestive process.
4. Feed according to: (a) age, (b) work being done, (c) size, (d) temperament.
5. Make no sudden changes in type of food or routine of feeding. All changes in diet must be gradual, spread over several days.
6. Feed at the same hours each day.
7. Feed only clean, good quality forage. Horses are fastidious feeders. Musty or dusty fodder can prove actually harmful.
8. Feed something succulent each day. Grass, sliced carrots, apples, etc.
9. When work starts, digestion stops. Blood needed to aid digestion goes instead to the lungs. Horses may do quiet work after a small feed, two to three pounds, but need complete rest after a large feed, four to six pounds, and should not be worked fast when the stomach is full of grass or hay. Average period of retention of food in the stomach is from one to one and a half hours.

Amounts to feed

Amounts fed will depend on: whether horse is kept stabled or at grass; size, age, and temperament of horse; what work he is doing; whether it is summer or winter; what items are available.

As an approximate guide an average size 16.0 h.h. horse requires a total weight of from 25 to 30 pounds of food a day. When hunting regularly, this might be approximately 10 to 14 pounds of oats with 18 to 14 pounds of hay per day.

Horses are great individualists and each one will vary from day to day. A good feeder will have the ability to see from day to day which horses do well and which do not and adjust their feeding accordingly. This requires talent, observation, and a love of and interest in animals.

Times to feed

Times of feeds will vary from stable to stable according to working conditions. Main rules are: feed little and often, always feed at the same hours each day, feed regularly—long periods of absence are harmful.

For example: First feed before exercise, small feed, 7 a.m. Second feed at mid-day, after exercise and strapping, larger feed. Third feed at night, largest feed.

If it is possible to feed four times a day, give the third feed, small feed, at 4 p.m. and fourth feed, largest feed, at night.

When not to feed

1. When horse is heated after work. Stomach is not then in proper state for digestion of food.
2. If horse is exhausted, after violent exercise. A gruel may be given at this time, as it is easily digestible. Allow horse to rest for an hour or two, then feed.
3. When horse is weakened from long fasting be particularly careful to feed only small quantities. Too much food under these conditions could produce indigestion and, in some cases, gastritis and colic. An over-hearty feed is always harmful. Feed small quantities at frequent intervals.

BIBLIOGRAPHY

Horse Breeding and Stud Management, Henry Wynmalen, ch. XII.

The Manual of Horsemanship, pp. 180-181 and 186-199.

First Aid Hints for the Horse Owner, W. E. Lyon, pp. 16-19.

Top Form Book of Horse Care, pp. 87-102.

CHAPTER 6

FEEDS — FORAGE

TYPES OF HAY

1. "Seed" Hay—seed sown as a rotation crop. It is spoken of as a one, two or three year "ley" depending on the length of time it is left undisturbed. Sainfoin or Timothy, Lucerne or Alfalfa, Clover and Mixture hay (comprising Timothy, rye grass, clovers and trefoil) are all "Seed" Hay.
2. "Meadow" Hay—cut from permanent pasture and usually contains a greater variety of grasses than "Seed" hay. Cocksfoot or orchard grass, sweet vernal, meadow fescue, rye grass and clover will all be found in good "Meadow" hay.

"Seed" hay is hard and is generally of higher feeding value than "Meadow" hay, which is soft. "Meadow" hay is more easily digested.

PROPERTIES OF GOOD HAY

1. A good aroma—"nose".
2. Sweet taste.
3. The colour of the flowering head should be retained until the hay is a year old.
4. It should be a good colour—greenish to brownish, but *not* yellow, this is a sign of weathering.
5. Crisp to the touch, bright and clean.
6. It should not be dusty or mouldy.
7. It should contain many of the good grasses, few of the inferior ones, and no bad ones. (See "Grasses".)
8. Should be cut when grasses are at their best—i.e., when they are still young, between the flower and the seed.

Note: "Seed" hay should preferably be in the stack twelve months before feeding to horses, and "Meadow" hay eighteen months. New hay, i.e., less than six months old is best avoided as it may prove indigestible.

41

QUALITY OF HAY

The quality and value of hay depend on:
1. The grasses of which it is composed.
2. The soil in which it has been grown.
3. The time of year when it was cut.
4. The way in which it has been saved, i.e., made.
5. Whether is it first or second cut. Second cut (aftermath) is inferior, consisting mainly of leaves and flowering heads.
6. How it has been stored.

MOWBURNT HAY

Hay which has deteriorated due to over-heating in the rick is known as "mowburnt". It is a yellow or dark brown colour. Cause—baling hay before juicy stems are dry.

WEEDS

Presence of weeds in hay usually signifies an impoverished state of the land on which the hay has been grown (lacking in heart). Avoid hay containing weeds.

GRASSES

Best grasses: Rye grass, Meadow Foxtail, Crested Dogstail, American Orchard (Coxfoot)—high in food value but not liked, Meadow Fescue, Timothy grass, Sweet Vernal, Blue Grass Fescue.
Inferior grasses: Smooth Meadow, Yorkshire fog.
Bad grasses: Common rush, Common meadow barley.

Timothy

Very commonly used hay for horses and probably the safest hay. Timothy is carbonaceous—fairly rich in carbohydrates and fats but lacking in digestible protein and minerals. Usually free from dust and mould.

Lucerne or Alfalfa

Lucerne (known as Alfalfa in America) is exceedingly rich in protein and has a high lime content. Very palatable. Best for horses when it is fairly mature before cutting. Care must be taken not to overfeed lucerne—about $\frac{1}{2}$ lb. per day for each 100 lbs. of live weight is safe; i.e., not more than 4 to 5 lbs. daily.

Clover

Ranks second to lucerne in feeding value. It is palatable, slightly laxative and has high protein and mineral content. Sometimes rather dusty.

Medium red clover is most commonly used as other varieties are usually coarse and large amounts are wasted. As with lucerne, feed only a limited amount daily. A mixture of clover and timothy hay is a very desirable combination.

DRIED GRASS

Grass is cut (usually only the best) and dried immediately. It loses very little of its original goodness and is an excellent feed for the winter months.

CHAFF

Chaff is chopped up hay. Only good hay must be used. Ideally chaff should be cut on the premises as bulk chaff purchased from feedstore is often composed of rubbish. Oat straw may also be used for chaff and is sometimes preferred by horses on maximum grain allowance since good hay chaff is too nutritious for the system to absorb. Adding chaff to grain feed ensures mastication of oats. Amount of chaff to be given—approximately one pound per feed.

BRAN (A by-product of the milling process of wheat)

A bulky, protein-rich concentrate. Bran should be broad in flake, dry and floury, not musty. Fed wet, or as a bran mash, bran has a cooling, laxative effect. Bran may be mixed with regular grain ration or it may replace the bulk of the grain on workless days. Often fed dry after horse has been given a physic to stop further action.

OATS

The best energising food for horses. Oats should be clean, hard, plump, heavy and sweet smelling. Bruising, rolling, crushing or crimping oats exposes the kernel to the digestive juices and thereby aids digestion. After three weeks crushed oats begin to lose their value. It is advisable to purchase whole oats and crush them on the premises, as required. Oats are deficient in calcium.

OTHER GRAINS

Barley

Used in many parts of the world as part or all of the grain ration for horses. For best results barley should be rolled or crimped as it is a very hard grain. Coarsely ground barley may be fed to horses but it is generally advisable to avoid grinding any grain feed. Any grinding, coarse or fine, produces dustiness. Grinding produces doughiness and digestive disturbances.

Boiled barley (often with a handful of linseed added before boiling) is a valuable addition to the weekly bran mash and will help to keep flesh on horses.

Wheat

Wheat is not suitable grain for horses. Very small quantities (not more than twenty per cent of the daily grain ration) may be fed, crushed or boiled, with oats or barley, or bran or chaff. Wheat has a high vitamin E content and is sometimes recommended for stallions and brood mares.

Maize (Corn)

A feed high in energy value but poor in proteins and minerals. Generally considered too heating and fattening to be fed in large amounts. Small amounts (up to twenty-five per cent of the grain ration) may be fed to horses in hard work. Corn may be fed shelled, on the cob, or flaked, but not ground.

PEAS AND BEANS

Very rich in protein, but heating and fattening. Peas and beans are fed split or kibbled, or crushed. Horses wintered out at grass may be fed up to six pounds of peas or beans per day with advantage. If mixing peas or beans with grain feed, mix one part beans to two part oats, by weight.

BOILED FOOD

Barley and oats may be fed boiled. Boiling or steaming softens the grain. Boiling has disadvantage of making oats absorb too much water, which in turn dilutes the digestive juices, thereby making the horse fat but also soft in condition. Steaming overcomes this difficulty—up to fifteen gallons of oats may be steamed with three to four gallons of water. Boiled or steamed grain tempts a difficult feeder, helps to keep flesh on horse, and helps to avoid constipation when fresh green food is not available.

GRASS MEAL

If of good quality may contain 19 per cent protein. Start with small quantity and work up to one pound per day. Feed damp, mixed with grain and bran.

DRIED SUGAR BEET PULP

Must never be fed dry as choking may easily result and dry pulp will swell within the stomach. Beet pulp should be soaked in plenty of water overnight. Feed mixed with bran and grain. Useful bulk feed for horses doing slower work—helps keep flesh on horses. Not suitable for horses used for hard, fast work.

HORSE AND PONY CUBES

Are a compound of a variety of ingredients including oats, barley, maize, bran, locust bean, linseed cake, groundnut meal, grass meal, molasses, etc., plus vitamins and minerals. Composition varies according to brand.

Cubes may be substituted in part or whole for grain ration and/or hay. Advantages include: ease of transportation, ease of storage, no mixing, ensures standardised, mixed, balanced diet with necessary vitamins and minerals included. Ponies fed cubes are less likely to "hot up" than those fed on grain. Disadvantages include: relative expense, danger that their low moisture content may lead to choking, unless adequate water is available. Chaff or bran fed with cubes ensures adequate mastication and salivation before swallowing.

ROOTS

Something succulent, i.e., green or juicy, makes the feed more appetising, gives bulk, provides variety and helps to satisfy the natural desire for grass.

Green Food

Grass or lucerne, etc., should be readily available in summer and may be fed either in a hay net or chaffed up with hay and added to the feed.

Carrots

Best of all roots. Feed only sound carrots. Feed whole or cut lengthwise. Carrots are cooling and are a natural remedy for some diseases. Carrots are easily digestible and are good for horses with respiratory diseases, coughs and broken wind. Three to four pounds per day will tempt delicate feeders.

Mangolds, Swedes and Turnips

Relished by horses, particularly in winter months. Scrub well under running tap, slice lengthwise or feed whole. Begin by feeding one or two pounds daily and increase to four pounds as horse becomes accustomed to them.

Some horses also enjoy parsnips and beetroots.

PREPARATION OF FOOD

Bran Mash

Use a metal or plastic bucket (not wood). To one third of a bucket of bran add as much boiling water as the bran will absorb. Add half an ounce of salt. Stir well with a stick. Cover to keep in steam and allow mash to steam until cool enough to feed. Correctly made, the mash should be "crumble-dry", not stiff and not thin and watery. The mash is more appetising if a handful of oats is added, or some treacle, or some molasses, or a pint of cooked linseed. Bran mash is usually fed the night before a rest day.

Linseed

Highly nutritious and rich in protein and oils. May be fed as "jelly" or "tea" to improve condition and give a gloss to the coat. Daily allowance is half to one pound of seed before cooking.

Linseed "jelly": Cover linseed with water and soak overnight. After twenty-four hours, add more water and bring to boil. Soaked, unboiled linseed may prove poisonous to horses. Allow to cool. Resulting jelly is then tipped out and mixed with evening feed. Linseed burns easily and should be cooked in an insulated boiler.

Linseed "tea": Prepared as above but with more water. The water in which the linseed is cooked is very nutritious and is employed with bran to make a linseed mash.

Linseed Oil Meal is also available and may be fed with carbonaceous grains or roughages. Has same properties as cooked linseed. Feed not more than one pound mixed with grain daily.

Soyabean Meal

Similar to linseed oil meal but has not been used extensively for horses. Feed in small quantities only (about one pound daily). Soyabean meal is often used in preparation of horse and pony cubes.

Clover Screenings

The dried leaves which have fallen back. Clover screenings are the most valuable part of clover hay, but should not be fed to horses in hard work.

Lucerne, Alfalfa, Sainfoin and Vetches

Cut as green meat—higher feeding value than pasture or clover hay. Feed in small amounts gradually increasing to eight pounds a day. A plot of Lucerne is a useful addition to any stable. It may be cut up to five times a year.

Cod Liver Oil

Excellent tonic for debility cases. Beneficial influence on formation of healthy bone. Good preventive for rickets and pulmonary affections. Feed one to two tablespoonfuls twice weekly.

Cod liver oil possesses a nasty taste and smell and may not be eaten readily. It is obtainable in the form of codolettes—soft, small cake—in which taste is camouflaged by addition of palatable spices. Codolettes are easily administered and readily eaten.

Milk

May be given with good results to horses in training. Feed either liquid or in powdered form. (Feed up to one gallon per day, mixed with bran and oats.)

Eggs (raw)

Excellent muscle builder and conditioner. Eggs contain an anti-vitamin and should not be fed constantly, but are a valuable addition to the diet of a horse in good condition. Feed six a day for three or four days.

Beer or Stout

Good tonic for horses in training. Give two bottles a day up to three days prior to competition.

47

Gruel

Made from oatmeal. Palatable and refreshing to a tired horse. Easily digestible.

Place a double handful of oatmeal in a bucket. Add a little cold water and stir well. (Cold water prevents lumps forming.) Pour on a gallon and a half of hot, not boiling, water and stir again. Offer when cool. Gruel should be thin enough for horse to drink. Boiling water should not be used as it produces a more starchy compound than is suitable for digestion by an exhausted horse.

Hay Tea

Prepared by steeping hay in boiling water and allowing the infusion to cool. Contains valuable nutrition material in the form of mineral salts and other soluble substances.

Salt

Small quantities are a necessary addition to a horse's feed. May be given as a "salt" or "mineral" lick, as a lump of "rock salt" in manger, or a teaspoonful added to feed once daily. First two methods preferable.

Warm Water

The oxygen is removed from water by heating and warm water is therefore flat. It is correct to provide artificially warmed water for an exhausted horse as cold water would be a shock to the system. Ice cold water, equally, is not desirable.

BIBLIOGRAPHY

Horse Breeding and Stud Management, H. Wynmalen, ch. XII and pp. 30-32 and 135-136.

First Aid Hints for the Horse Owner, Lt.-Col. W. E. Lyon, pp. 16-19.

The Manual of Horsemanship, B.H.S., pp. 181-186.

Top Form Book of Horse Care, Frederick Harper, ch. 10.

Horsemen's Veterinary Adviser, Joseph B. Davidson, D.V.M., pp. 203-212.

CHAPTER 7

SADDLERY

CARE

1. Saddlery, called "tack", should be kept clean and in good repair.
2. All "tack" should be inspected periodically and minor defects remedied. Particular attention should be paid to stitching, which will rot or break before leather.
3. Leather will dry out and crack unless it is kept soft with oil or fat. Glycerine, Olive oil, and Castor oil are good for leather. Neatsfoot oil will rot leather and come off on hands and clothing. The best saddle soap contains all necessary glycerine or oil to keep tack in regular use pliable.
4. If tack is to be stored—cover with Vaseline.
5. Do not wash leather with soda or hot water. Do not place close to artificial heat.
6. Hang up saddle and bridle immediately upon removal from horse. This allows air to get to saddle lining, and avoids possible damage to tack thrown carelessly down.

THE SADDLE—STRUCTURE

1. The frame on which a saddle is built is called a "tree". It is made, traditionally, of beech wood, but many modern trees are made of laminated wood, bonded under pressure and then moulded.
2. The "tree" may be broken if the saddle is dropped, or if horse rolls with saddle on. A broken "tree" will injure the horse's back. If in doubt, have saddle checked by saddler.
3. The saddle should be so shaped that it assists the rider to sit in its central and lowest part.
4. A saddle may have either a full panel or a half panel.
   Full Panel: Reaches almost to bottom of saddle flap and is lined all the way down. A full panel saddle has only a short sweat-flap between panel and girth tabs.

Half Panel: Reaches half way down saddle flap. A half panel
saddle has a large sweat-flap reaching almost to the
bottom of the saddle flap.

5. Most stirrup bars are hinged to allow the point to be turned
up to prevent stirrup leathers slipping off when a saddled
horse is led. When the horse is being ridden the points should
always be down.

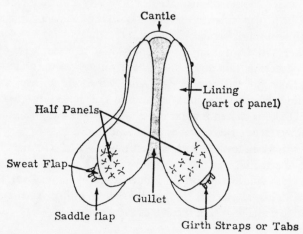

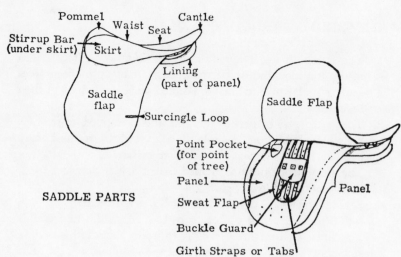

SADDLE PARTS

SADDLE LININGS

There are three kinds of saddle linings:

1. Leather: Long lasting if well kept.

2. Serge: Absorbent, but does not wear well. Hard to keep clean.

3. Linen.   Easy to wipe clean. Dries quickly, wears longer than serge but not as long as leather.

FITTING A SADDLE

1. Weight must be evenly distributed on the back muscles.
2. No weight on loins.
3. No pressure on horse's spine (test with rider mounted).
4. Front arch not too low or too wide. With rider mounted hand should pass easily under front arch.
5. Front arch not too narrow. The withers must not be pinched.
6. Movement of shoulder blades must not be hampered.
7. Panel must be correctly stuffed. Stuffing should be regulated to give support for the knee and be tilted to prevent rider sliding backwards.
8. Once a year, saddle should be checked by a saddler who will test the tree, stitching, and re-stuff as necessary.

STANDING AND CARRYING A SADDLE

1. Stand saddle on front arch. Fold girth to protect pommel from rough ground.
2. Avoid placing saddle on the ground if possible. Leather is easily torn and scratched by rough surfaces.
3. If saddle must be placed on ground, put it where it will not be knocked over by people or horses.
4. A saddle should be carried:
   (a) With the front arch in the crook of the elbow (this allows the bridle to be carried on the same shoulder and leaves other hand free).
   (b) On the head.
   (c) Along the thigh, with the hand in the front arch.

The above methods prevent injury to the cantle against walls and doorways.

MATERIALS REQUIRED FOR TACK CLEANING

1. A saddle horse.
2. Cleaning bracket suspended from wall or ceiling.
3. Bucket of cold or tepid water.
4. Two sponges: one large for washing, one small, flat one known as an "elephant ear sponge" for saddle soap.
5. A chamois leather, for drying.
6. Bar of glycerine or tin of saddle soap.
7. Two stable rubbers: one dry to cover the clean saddle, one for drying metal work.
8. Dandy brush for cleaning sweat from serge linings.
9. Metal polish, and an old cloth for applying it.
10. Burnisher, for rubbing up metal work after using metal polish.

Dandy Brush

Horse Hair Pad

Cleaning Hook

Bucket

Stable Rubbers

Chamois

Polish Cloth

Sponges

Saddle Horse

Glycerine Soap

CLEANING A SADDLE

1. Place saddle on saddle horse.
2. Remove girths, stirrup leathers and irons, and girth buckle guards.
3. Clean lining:

    Leather: Remove all dirt. Hold saddle, pommel down, over bucket, and wash, using large sponge. Squeeze excess water from sponge before use. Try to avoid water running under lining and saturating stuffing. Dry lining with chamois (never used dry but always well wrung out). Apply saddle soap.

    Linen: Sponge off (scrub if necessary) keeping as dry as possible. Stand saddle up to dry. Do not place it near a fire or hot radiator.

    Serge: Lining must be dry before cleaning. Brush well with dandy brush. If very dirty, lining may be scrubbed, but it will take several days to dry.

4. Replace saddle on saddle horse and wash all leather work thoroughly. Rinse sponge frequently in bucket and squeeze out well. Avoid getting leather too wet. Dry with chamois. All small black accumulations of grease and dirt, known as "jockeys", should have been removed. Never use a sharp instrument to remove "jockeys". If difficulty is encountered, rub them off with a small pad of horse hair.

5. Rinse out "'elephant ear" sponge and squeeze it as dry as possible. Dip glycerine bar in water and soap sponge liberally. Using circular movement, soap all leather work: panel, girth tabs, sweat flap, underside of saddle flap, outer side of saddle flap, underside of skirt, outer side of skirt and seat. Pay particular attention to all stitching—liberal soaping will keep thread supple and lengthen its life. Do not use soap on top of dirt.

6. Wash and dry stirrup irons. Clean all metal work with metal polish. Rub up with burnisher.

7. Cover saddle with dry stable rubber and put away in a dry place.

8. Stirrup leathers and leather girths should be treated in the same way as the leather parts of the saddle. Clean buckles with metal polish.

9. Before using saddle again, the seat and outside flaps may be rubbed over with a moist sponge and dried with a chamois, to remove dust and surplus soap which might stain breeches.

"PUTTING UP" A SADDLE

1. Place saddle on bracket, about eighteen inches long, attached to saddle room wall at a convenient height.
2. Hang stirrup irons on hook underneath saddle bracket.
3. Hang girth, stirrup leathers, and martingale on hooks alongside saddle bracket.

NUMNAHS (SADDLE PADS)

1. Made of leather, felt, sorbo rubber, sheepskin, or nylon fabric, cut to the shape of a saddle.
2. Attached to one girth tab on either side, above girth buckle, by a leather or web loop; or by an adjustable strap round saddle panel.
3. Objects of numnahs:
   (a) to rectify badly stuffed or ill-fitting saddle.
   (b) to protect unfit horse's back.
   (c) to protect the spine of a jumper (by ensuring it does not contact gullet of saddle during jump).
   If used to rectify ill-fitting saddle, numnah is an emergency measure and saddle should be re-stuffed, or replaced by one that fits.
4. Numnah should be slightly larger than saddle. When in place it should be visible for about one inch all round.
5. To avoid pressure being borne on the wither or spine, pull numnah up into front arch of saddle before tightening girths.
6. Cleaning: *Leather*. Clean as for all other leather. If storing, cover well with vegetable oil or Vaseline. Soften with oil again before use.

   Sponge or rubber. Wash with pure soap or animal wash. Avoid using synthetic detergents on horses or horse clothing.

   Felt and all types sheepskin. Dry and brush hard with dandy brush. Scrub if necessary. Air well and guard against moth. Some nylon fabric or synthetic sheepskin numnahs may be washed in washing machine. Use pure soap. Hang out to dry in warm, airy room.

FELT SADDLES OR PAD SADDLES

1. Made of felt. Sometimes covered, or partially covered with leather.

2. May have a tree forepart, or steel arch, which will help to keep it straight on the pony. Otherwise felt saddles have no tree.
3. Felt saddles often have web girth permanently attached. For safety they should have two straps and buckles, or two web girths.
4. Some felt saddles have "D's" instead of stirrup bars. Safety stirrups (with rubber band at outside) should be employed on these saddles.
5. A crupper may be necessary to prevent felt saddle slipping forward on a fat pony.

WITHER PADS

1. Used to prevent pressure of the front arch of the saddle on horse's withers.
2. Made of woollen or cloth material. May be improvised by folding a stable rubber.
3. Wither pads are emergency measures only. Saddle should be re-stuffed, or changed, so that it fits properly.

GIRTHS *Types*

Web: Do not wear well. Are liable to snap without warning. For this reason two should always be used together.

Leather: Excellent for use on fit horse. May gall soft horse, even when kept clean and soft. There are many types of straight, shaped and cross-over leather girths. The three fold is most popular. A strip of well-oiled flannel should be kept in the fold to keep girth soft.

String: Good, general purpose girth. Easy to keep clean but temporarily shrink after washing. Air can circulate and so help

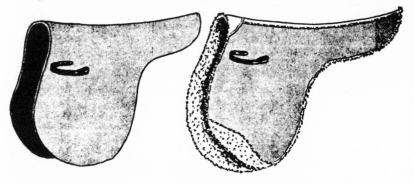

Felt Numnah   Sheepskin Numnah

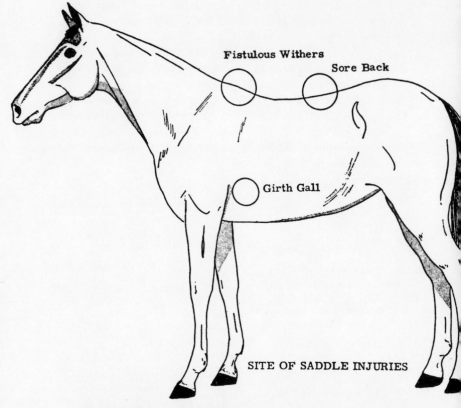

Fistulous Withers

Sore Back

Girth Gall

SITE OF SADDLE INJURIES

prevent galling. Do not slip on unclipped horse. Last longer than web, but not so long as leather.

Nylon: Similar to string but harder wearing. Liable to slip more than string. Stretch with use.

Mohair: Similar to string but much softer. Ideal for use on soft, unfit horse. Prevents galling.

Fitting

Girth should not be too short or too long. When drawn up for first mounting, buckles should reach at least to second hole on each side, and there should be at least two spare holes above buckles on each side.

Cleaning

Leather: Wash, dry and soap as described under 'cleaning a saddle'. Clean buckles. Oil inside of 3-fold leather girth occasionally—do not use mineral (motor) oil.

Web, String, Nylon and Mohair: Brush daily with dandy brush. Wash occasionally using pure soap. Rinse thoroughly.

STIRRUP IRONS

1. Should be of best quality metal. Hand-forged stainless steel is safest and most satisfactory. Plated metal flakes easily, pure nickel is too soft.
2. Fitting: with the broadest part of rider's foot in the stirrup, there should be half an inch clearance at each side. If stirrup is too small rider's foot may be jammed, if too large, foot may slip through.
3. Cleaning: wash and dry thoroughly. Clean all metals, except plain steel, with metal polish and shine with a dry rubber. Clean plain steel with metal polish and silver sand, and shine with a dry rubber.
4. Safety stirrups: those most generally used are metal with rubber band at one side. Rubber band must be worn on the outside. Disadvantages—due to being weighted more on one side than the other they do not hang straight. Rubber band may come undone or break.

BRIDLES

Parts of a snaffle bridle

1. Head piece and throat lash made on the same piece of leather.
2. Brow band.
3. Two cheek pieces, attached at one end to the head piece and at the other to the bit.
4. Nose band, on its own head piece.
5. Bit—attached to the cheek pieces and reins by stitches, or by studs or buckles if they are required to be detachable. Stitched "mount" looks best for shunting and showing. Studded "mount" is useful for exercising as different bits may be attached, and it is easier to clean. Buckled "mount" is clumsy and ugly.
6. Reins—may be plain, plaited, or laced leather with a centre buckle.

Parts of a double bridle

Same as for a snaffle bridle, plus:
1. Additional and separate cheek pieces for the bridoon.
2. Two bits—bridoon (thin snaffle) and curb bit.

3. Additional pair of reins—bridoon rein is usually slightly the wider and reins are of plain leather.
4. Curb chain, attached by a hook on each of the upper rings of the bit. It has a special link ("fly" link) in the centre through which the lip strap passes.
5. Lip strap—narrow leather strap, made in two parts, which attach to the "D"s on either side of the cheek of the bit.

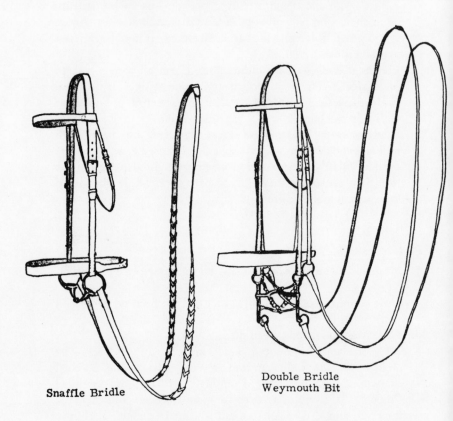

Snaffle Bridle

Double Bridle
Weymouth Bit

FITTING A BRIDLE

1. Throat lash: should be done up to allow the full width of an adult hand between it and the side of the jaw bone. Should never be tight.
2. Brow band: should lie below the ears, not touching them. Should not interfere with the hang of the head piece. Prevents head piece from slipping back.

3. Cavesson nose-band: should be half way between the projecting cheekbone and the corners of the mouth. Should be loose enough to admit two fingers between the nose-band and the horse's nose.
4. Dropped nose-band: must be carefully fitted. The front should be well above the nostrils and the back fits in the chin groove. Should be tight enough to prevent horse crossing his jaw, but not so tight as to prevent flexing of the jaw.
5. Bridoon and bit: should not be so high that they wrinkle the lips, nor so low that they touch the teeth. Bits of the correct width for the mouth must always be used. A bit that is too narrow will pinch, and one too wide will bruise the corners of the mouth when moving from side to side. The bridoon should be above the bit.
6. Curb chain: should be flat against the chin when in use. Attach one end to the offside hook. From the near side, twist the chain to the right until it is flat. Place the base of the link needed for correct fitting on the near side hook, with the thumb uppermost. Curb chain should come into action when the cheeks of the bit are drawn back to an angle of 45 degrees with the mouth.
7. Lip strap: should pass through the "fly" link on the curb chain; should not be tight. Purposes: to hold curb chain if it becomes unhooked, to prevent horse catching hold of the cheeks of the bit, and to prevent the cheeks of a Banbury-action bit, which are not fixed, from revolving forward and up.
8. Check under all head pieces to ensure that they are flat and to smooth the mane. If adjustment is necessary to the nose-band headpiece, ease it up at the poll and then ease it down the other side. Stand in front of horse to check that everything is straight, the bit, or bits, are level in the mouth, and that all keepers are firm—no flapping ends.

CLEANING A BRIDLE

1. Hang up bridle on a hook. Take off the nose band, let out the cheek pieces to the lowest hole. Bridle should be taken apart and cleaned about once a week, when all stitching may be checked.
2. Wash and dry bit or bits. (Remove curb chain to wash and polish.)

3. Wash all leatherwork and dry with a chamois—as described under 'Cleaning a Saddle'.
4. Polish bits and buckles as described for 'Stirrup irons'.
5. Soap all leatherwork, remembering the importance of the underside. Wrap sponge around the straps and rub gently up and down.
6. When cleaning the bridle on the hook, hold it with one hand to keep it taut and clean with the other. When cleaning the reins, step backwards, away from the hook, to keep them taut. Work downwards, towards buckle. Hang reins on another hook to keep them clean.
7. Put the bridle together, replacing all buckles in their correct holes, with strap ends into their keepers and runners.
('Keepers' are stitched loops; 'runners' are loops that slide up and down.)

"PUTTING UP" A BRIDLE

1. Hang bridle on hook. Take buckle in centre of reins in one hand and hold just behind and slightly above nose band.
2. Pass throat lash (long end) across in front of the bridle, round the back, through loop of reins (at buckle), round the front of the bridle again and fasten to its end hole. This gives 'figure eight' appearance.
3. Put nose band right around the outside of the cheek pieces. Do not buckle but pass strap end through keepers.
4. Twist curb chain flat and hook across the front of the bit.
5. Bridle may also be correctly "put-up" by passing throat lash directly through the loop of the reins without forming a 'figure of eight' and then wrapping nose band around outside of bridle.
6. When "put-up", hang bridle on bridle hanger which is either half-moon or round in shape, in order to keep headpiece in the correct shape.
7. If bridle hanger is sufficiently high up, reins may be left hanging straight down tack room wall.

MARTINGALES

1. Standing martingale: A strap attached at one end to the nose band and at the other, between the horse's forelegs to the girth, supported by a neck strap. Never attach to dropped nose band.

Purpose: To prevent horse from raising his head beyond the angle of control.

Fitting: With horse's head up in correct position, place a hand underneath the martingale and push it up. It should just reach into the horse's gullet.

2. Running martingale: A strap attached at one end between the horse's forelegs to the girth. The other end divides into two straps, each with a ring at the end. The reins are passed through these rings. The martingale is supported by a neck strap. Leather 'stops' should be used on the reins between the rings of the martingale and the bit.

   Purpose: to prevent the horse raising his head above the angle of control, or throwing it from side to side.

   Fitting: When attached to the girth, take both rings up one side of the horse's shoulder. They should reach to the withers.

   Note: The neck strap should fit so that it will admit a hand at the withers. The buckle should be on the near side.

3. Irish martingale: two metal rings connected by a leather strap four to six inches long.

   Purpose: to keep the reins in place, preventing them from going over the horse's head. Used mainly in racing.

   Fitting: the snaffle reins pass through the rings, beneath the horse's neck.

BREASTPLATES

Hunting type breastplate: a neck strap attached to the front "D"s of the saddle on each side of the wither, and to the girth between the forelegs.

   Purpose: prevents saddle from slipping back.

   Fitting: the neck strap should admit a hand at the withers. The straps joined to the girth and the "D"s should be flat, without strain, when breastplate is in its proper position. If a martingale is necessary as well as a breastplate, attachments for either standing or running martingale can be added to the breast ring.

Aintree type: web or elastic strap fits across the breast and attaches to the girth straps under the saddle flaps. Leather strap across the neck in front of the withers holds the breast strap in position. Breast strap must not be fitted so high as to restrict the freedom of the neck.

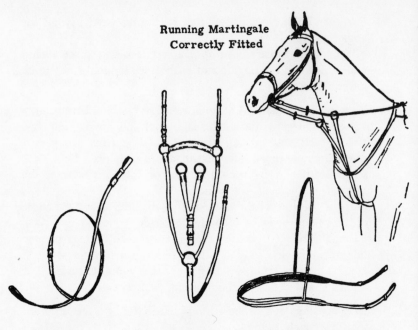

Running Martingale
Correctly Fitted

Standing
Martingale

Hunting
Breastplate
with
Running Martingale
Attachment

Aintree Type Breastplate
(racing)

Polo breastplate: similar to Aintree type but made of leather. Has a loop set on the inside in the centre of the breast strap through which the standing martingale passes.

CRUPPER

Leather strap attached to back "D" of saddle and passing under tail.

Purpose: prevent saddle from slipping forward.

Fitting: must be put on when girth is loose or undone. Stand close to near hind leg, gather up tail in right hand and pass it through the crupper. Draw crupper well up to top of tail, and smooth all the hairs. Adjust length of crupper so that it steadies the saddle. It should not be so short that it pulls the tail up.

BIBLIOGRAPHY

The Manual of Horsemanship, B.H.S., pp. 87-115.
Saddlery, by E. Hartley Edwards, chapters 3, 7, 14, 15 and 18.
Stitch by Stitch, by Diana R. Tuke.
Bit by Bit, by Diana R. Tuke.

CHAPTER 8

THE BACK AND SADDLE FITTING

PARTS CONCERNED

1. Withers.
2. Shoulders.
3. Girth.
4. Loins.
5. Spine.

THE WITHERS

1. Should be well moulded and well clothed at the sides by muscle.
2. Provide an anchorage for a number of muscles which attach the scapula (shoulder blade bone) to the body.
3. The height of the withers provides a prominence which helps to give a seating to the saddle.
4. Withers which extend well back are essential for a well-laid-back scapula.
5. Thin, high withers make saddle fitting difficult.

SHOULDERS

1. Should be of a good length, with ample slope.
2. Degree of inclination of good shoulder, measured from point of shoulder to junction of neck and withers, should be approximately sixty degrees. From point of shoulder to centre of withers (highest point), the angle should be forty-three degrees. From point of shoulder to junction of withers and back, the angle should be forty degrees.
3. The angle formed between the scapula and the humerus, at the scapulohumeral joint may vary between 110 degrees and 130 degrees.
4. The degree of slope of the humerus is important. It may vary according to relative length of humerus and whether the elbow and fore-arm are set on well forward or well back. The elbow of the Thoroughbred lies farther forward than that of an indigenous pony.

63

5. A well-inclined shoulder gives free range of extension and flexion which improves action and increases the potential speed.
6. A well-inclined shoulder provides room for adequate muscular development. Good length of muscle is important.
7. Sloping shoulder is main anti-concussion device within fore-limb. It lessens the jar as the weight falls on the fore-foot.

THE SPINE

1. Composed of a chain of bones, each capable of very slight movement both up and down and from side to side.
2. The bony processes growing from the upper part of each vertebra (bone in the chain) form the ridge of the backbone. These processes are the seat of bone trouble which may be found in a sore back.
3. There must be no pressure on the spine from the saddle. Nor must the saddle pinch the spine (press the flesh against the bone). Pinching is not evident for two or three days but eventually causes swelling and possibly an abscess.

THE BACK

1. Extends from the withers to the quarters. It contains and is supported by eighteen thoracic vertebræ, carrying eighteen pairs of ribs, and six lumbar vertebræ, which lie behind the space occupied by the saddle.
2. Back should be shaped in such a way that the saddle will stay on it, will not slip forward or backward.
3. Should show a definite line and contour. Should never be arched and only slightly concave.
4. A 'roach-back' shortens the horse's stride. Gives an uncomfortable ride.
5. A 'sway' back throws an additional strain on the back muscles.

THE RIBS

1. Eight pairs of 'true' ribs—attached to the breast bone (sternum).
2. Ten pairs of 'false' ribs—carried by the ten rear thoracic vertebræ and not directly attached to the sternum.
3. The ribs project a few inches on either side of the vertebræ before curving downwards.

4. The weight of the saddle must rest on the muscle covering these horizontal parts, and nowhere else.
5. Some weight can be borne on the slopes of the front ribs which are stouter and fixed into the sternum. If weight is taken too low down—particularly with a slab-sided horse—breathing may be impeded.
6. The girth should not be too far forward, nor too tight, since the ribs behind the shoulder blades are capable of only slight movement as the horse inhales.

THE LOINS

1. That part of the back behind the saddle, containing the six lumbar vertebræ.
2. The loins are not protected by any ribs and should not support any weight.

SHOULDER BLADES

1. The forelegs are fitted to the trunk by large masses of muscle.
2. When forelegs move, shoulder blade bones move.
3. Any constriction by too tight fitting saddle on shoulder blade bone will affect the stride.
4. To test for constriction—lift foreleg by point of hoof, draw it forward. It should be possible then to get the fingers between the saddle and the shoulder.

CAUSES OF SORE BACKS

Pressure: stops the flow of blood, capillaries die and a lump of dead tissue forms.
Friction: the outer protecting scales of skin are rubbed off more quickly than they can be replaced; i.e., excess of wear over production. (Can also happen in the horse's mouth.)
Pressure and Friction caused by:
1. Poorly fitted saddle.
2. Improper saddling (panel flap turned under or wrinkled, etc.)
3. Dirty saddle lining.
4. Dirty or badly folded saddle blanket.
5. Careless riding—rolling or lounging in the saddle.
6. Unevenly placed loads.
7. Incorrectly fitted rollers.
8. Poor conformation.

PREVENTION OF SORE BACKS

1. Ensure that adjustment of saddle is correct.
   (a) Withers must not be pinched or pressed upon.
   (b) Saddle must allow absolute freedom of shoulder blades.
   (c) Loins should bear no weight.
   (d) All weight should be borne on the spring of the ribs. No pressure on spine.
   (e) There should be a clear channel of air along the spine.
2. Keep saddle lining clean.
3. If saddle blanket is used, ensure that it is clean and correctly folded. Saddle cloths and blankets must be very carefully put on or they will bear on the spine and at least cut out the channel of air.
4. A wither pad is only an emergency measure. When used it should be pushed up into the arch of the saddle and not allowed to press on the withers or the spine.
5. Rider must sit erect in the saddle at all times.
6. All stable clothing should be kept clean and should be carefully fitted. Rollers should be correctly adjusted to avoid pressure.
7. Before subjecting the horse's back to anything but short periods of pressure, it must be conditioned and hardened gradually.

TYPES OF SADDLE LINING

1. Leather: Long lasting, easy to clean, but can be hard on a back during a long day's hunting.
2. Linen: Similar to leather but slightly softer. More care is needed in washing.
3. Serge: Absorbent, does not wear well. Hard to keep clean. Good for cold days or on thin coated horse. Must be thoroughly brushed after use.

NUMNAHS

Made of a variety of fabrics including sheepskin, felt and nylon. Attached to saddle by strap. Care must be taken to ensure they fit the horse's back and are put on without wrinkles and without pressing on the spine. Can cause overheating of back and predispose it to soreness but are useful on some thin skinned horses.

CARE OF BACK ON REMOVAL OF SADDLE

1. Do not remove saddle immediately if horse is hot or back sweaty.
2. The flow of blood to the parts on which the saddle bears is stopped by the pressure of the saddle. Sudden removal of the saddle causes blood to rush back into the blood vessels and they may be ruptured.
3. Slacken the girth and leave the saddle in place for a while, allowing the blood to run slowly back into the blood vessels.
4. After removing the saddle, massage and slap the back gently to help restore normal circulation.
5. Remove saddle mark by spongeing with warm water, walking dry and then brushing, if weather is suitable. If spongeing is undesirable due to weather conditions, brush saddle mark off when back is dry.
6. If a horse is exposed to hot sunshine with an unwashed, sweating back, the back may be scalded.
7. The horse changes shape during the period he is in work and the amount of muscle on the back will vary. Saddle padding may have to be altered to accommodate changes in the shape of the back.

MEASURING BACK FOR CORRECT SADDLE FITTING

1. Take a piece of soft lead or stout electric cable eighteen inches long.
2. Shape cable over the withers approximately where the head of the saddle would lie and press well down.
3. Remove cable from horse and trace shape obtained on to a piece of paper, marking which is the 'near' and which the 'off' side.
4. Repeat procedure to obtain a measurement nine inches further back.
5. Take a final measurement along the length of the back from the withers.

TREATMENT OF SADDLE SORES AND GIRTH GALLS

1. Remove the cause. Note causes of sore backs, above. Girth galls are caused by working fat or unfit horse, badly fitted girth, dirt or dried sweat on horse in girth area.

2. Use nylon, mohair or Balding girth on unfit horses. Wrap girth with motorcycle tube, sheepskin, or cotton wool.
3. Stop work. If there is an open wound apply zinc and calamine ointment to take out soreness.
4. Don't allow horse to roll if in danger of opening wound.
5. When skin has healed, apply lead lotion or salt and water to harden skin.

NOTE—PREVENTION IS BETTER THAN CURE

Saddle up correctly. Place saddle on horse quietly, well forward of the wither and slide it gently back into position. Mount correctly. Hold the mane in the left hand and the front arch or the far side of the seat of the saddle where it joins the flap with the right hand. Do not put your hand on the cantle. Holding the cantle of a spring tree saddle may twist the spring, upset the balance of the saddle and cause a sore back.

BIBLIOGRAPHY

Saddlery, by E. Hartley Edward, ch. 15.
Horses In Action, R. H. Smythe, chapters 5 and 8.
Horsemen's Veterinary Adviser, Joseph B. Davidson, D.V.M., pp. 76-77.
The Manual of Horsemanship, B.H.S., pp. 93-94, 98-100.
Stitch by Stitch, by Diana R. Tuke.

CHAPTER 9

FITTING OF HALTERS AND BRIDLES AND BITTING

HEADCOLLARS AND HALTERS

Headcollars and halters should fit correctly.

Headband: Should rest flat just behind the ears and hang parallel just behind the projecting cheek bones.

Noseband: Should be two fingers' width below projecting cheek bones and admit two fingers between it and the horse's nose.

Brow band: Should be short enough to prevent headband from slipping down the neck, but long enough to avoid chafing the base of the ears.

Throat lash: Prevents head piece from slipping over the ears but should be quite loose. Throat lash should admit four fingers between it and cheek bones with head in normal position.

Leather
Headcollar

Halter with Non-Slip Knot

Rope Halters: Should be fitted to the horse's head and then the lead rope should be knotted at the noseband to avoid undue tightening caused by slip knot.

BRIDLES

The above remarks apply also to the Headband, Noseband, Brow band and Throat lash of bridles. In addition:

Bridoon: Should fit snugly into corners of mouth without wrinkling them. Correct width is important.

Bit: Lies one inch above the tush of a horse, two inches above the corner teeth of a mare. Must not be too narrow—nor too wide, for mouth.

Curb chain: Should be twisted right handed until it lies flat and smooth in the chin groove. Put the base of the link over the nearside hook. Curb chain should come into action when the cheeks of the bit are drawn back to an angle of 40 to 50 degrees with the mouth. The fly link (spare ring in centre of chain) should be on the underneath of the chain.

Lip strap: Passes through fly link (centre ring) of curb chain. Should be fairly loose. Allows curb chain to stay flat. Holds chain if it becomes unhooked.

NOTES ON BITTING—PRINCIPLES OF BITTING

1. Application of pressure on the horse's mouth.
2. Horse giving way to pressure by relaxing the jaw.
3. Instantaneous acknowledgment by yielding of the rider's hand.

The ability to control a horse by a bit is accomplished only by a system of correction and reward. When the horse obeys the action of the bit, the rider must yield to him at once.

Structure of the Horse's Mouth

1. Upper and lower jaw—longitudinal channels.
2. Bottom of lower jaw channel formed by group of muscles to which the tongue is attached.
3. Top of upper jaw channel formed by the palate.
4. Tongue lies in channel of lower jaw, and can move within mouth cavity while the mouth is closed.
5. The jawbones, the gums, are covered with thin layer of flesh and skin.
6. Teeth—incisors in the front of the mouth. Pair of 'tusks' or 'tushes' close behind the incisors. Toothless part of jaws, called the bars, follows before the molars commence.
7. The bars—gums—are the jawbone covered with a thin layer of flesh and skin, in which there is a mass of nerves. When these nerves are once destroyed, feeling will disappear.

Action of the Snaffle

1. On the tongue.
2. On the outside of the bars of the mouth.
3. On the lips, or the corners of the mouth.

Purpose of the Snaffle

Used in conjunction with rider's legs to teach horse to accept the bit with a still and correct head and supple jaw.

Types of Snaffle

1. Unjointed, half-moon or mullen mouth snaffle. Made of rubber, vulcanite or metal. Very mild.
2. Jointed Snaffle. Produces a squeezing or nut-cracker action in the mouth. Slightly more severe than mullen mouthpiece. Many varieties of jointed snaffle include: Eggbut snaffle (prevents pinching of the corners of the mouth), Dee cheek snaffle, normal cheek snaffle, Fulmer snaffle or Australian loose ring cheek snaffle (loose rings allow play in mouthpiece. Horse can mouth the bit and make saliva which relaxes the jaw), German snaffle (thick, mild mouthpiece and wire ring). Also snaffles with a link or spatula in the centre; nutcracker action is lessened.
3. Gag Snaffle. Usually a jointed mouthpiece is used. Rounded leather cheekpiece of bridle passes through holes in the top and bottom of snaffle rings. Has an upward, head raising effect.

Action of the Bit

1. On the bars of the mouth.
2. On the tongue.
3. Leverage action on lower jaw dependent on length of cheeks of bit and curb chain.

Purpose of the Bit

Used in conjunction with the bridoon (snaffle with thinner mouthpiece than described above), curb chain and lip strap forming a 'Double Bridle' or 'Full Bridle'.

Double Bridle permits rider to use more refined and imperceptible aid on trained horse. Helps to maintain a relaxed jaw.

Curb bit should not be used without bridoon since constant pressure on lower jaw will numb the mouth

Types of Bit

1. Weymouth bit with sliding mouthpiece—most common.
2. Weymouth bit with fixed mouthpiece—action is more direct.
3. Banbury bit—round bar mouthpiece is tapered in the centre to allow room for tongue. Mouthpiece fits into slots in the cheek which allows it to revolve and also to move up and down. Intention is to allow horse to mouth the bit and prevent him catching hold of it.

The Pelham

1. Is a combination of the curb and bridoon in one mouthpiece.
2. Numerous variations of mouthpiece, but generally speaking action is achieved by pressure on corners of mouth when top rein is used and on the poll and curb groove when bottom rein is used.
3. Sometimes used with leather 'converters' or 'roundings' and only one rein. Apart from the advantage of only one rein in child's hands there is no good reason for using a Pelham this way. Adds to the confusion of a bit already trying to do too many things at once.

The Kimblewick

1. Pelham type bit—an adaptation of a Spanish jumping bit.
2. Squared eye (as opposed to usual rounded one) allows more downward pressure on the Poll.
3. When hand is held low the Kimblewick will lower the horse's head very effectively.
4. Has the advantage of a single rein. Useful bit for children riding rather strong ponies.
5. If overemployed may make horse hang on the bit and the hand.

CAUSES OF RESISTANCE OR EVASION

1. Fear and pain—either present or in memory.
   (a) Tongue over the bit.
   (b) "Under the bit" (horse puts his head up).
   (c) Behind the bit (horse tucks head in).
   (d) Over the bit.

2. Bit injury or bruised or torn bars.
3. Wolf teeth. (Molar type teeth with little root, occurring in the upper jaw, just in front of the molars. See "wolf teeth," chapter 19.)
4. Severe bits.
5. Sharp teeth (when teeth need floating, i.e., rasping, see chapter 19, the skin may be pinched between teeth and bit).
6. Any discomfort.
   (a) Bit too narrow.
   (b) Rough edges (watch nickel bits for roughness).
   (c) Drop noseband wrongly fitted.
   (d) Brow band too narrow, pinching base of ears (horse will shake his head).
7. Horse incapable of doing what is asked (insufficient training).

BIBLIOGRAPHY

Saddlery, E. Hartley Edwards, chapters 3, 4, 6, 7, 8, 10, 11 and 12.

The Manual of Horsemanship, B.H.S., pp. 23-31 and 104-114.

Dressage, Henry Wynmalen, ch. 5.

Horsemanship, Waldemar Seunig, pp. 218-224.

Bit by Bit, Diana R. Tuke.

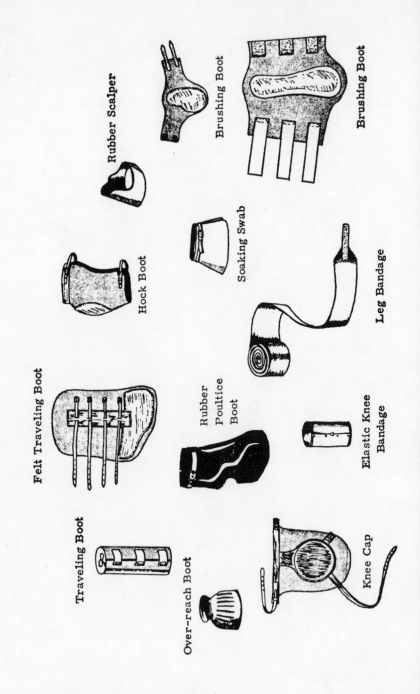

Rubber Scalper

Brushing Boot

Brushing Boot

Hock Boot

Soaking Swab

Leg Bandage

Felt Traveling Boot

Rubber Poultice Boot

Elastic Knee Bandage

Traveling Boot

Over-reach Boot

Knee Cap

74

CHAPTER 10

BOOTS, BANDAGES AND RUGS

BOOTS—PURPOSES, TYPES AND FITTING

Purposes

1. Protection of legs from injury by:
   (a) blows—jumping fixed fences, etc.
   (b) brushing—inside of leg near fetlock is knocked by opposite foot.
   (c) speedy cutting—inside of leg near knee is knocked by opposite foot.
   (d) over-reaching—toe of hind shoe striking heel of front foot.
2. Support of tendons of forelegs.
3. Treatment of injuries—i.e., poultice boot, etc.

Types

1. Shin boot—for both fore and hind legs. Eliminates danger of rapped shins in jumpers. Useful for racing over fences and show jumping.
2. Knee boot—"Carter" pattern or "Skeleton" kneecap. Protects knees of young horses schooling over fixed timber.
3. Coronet boot—mainly for protection during polo.
4. Polo boots—various types, usually similar to above but made of quarter-inch or half-inch felt. Usually larger than normal patterns with strong elastic insert to give tighter fit and more support.
5. Brushing boots—many different types. Lighter than polo boots. Rubber ring anti-brushing device. Yorkshire boot.
6. Speedicut boot—similar to brushing boots but fitted higher on leg. French pattern chasing boot also effective as speedicut boot.
7. Heel boot—protects point of fetlock which may come into contact with the ground during fast work or jumping.

8. Over-reach boot—rubber "bell" shaped boot fitting snugly round lower portion of pastern usually effective.
9. Tendon boot—made with strong pad at rear shaped to leg. Affords protection from high over-reach and strong support to weak tendons.
10. Hock boot—thick felt or leather. Protect hocks while travelling.
11. Travelling kneecaps—protect knees while travelling. Must be carefully fitted not to hinder knee movement.
12. "Pricker" boot—studded with tacks. Covers bandages and prevents horse tearing them off. Too dangerous, not recommended.
13. Poultice boot—accommodates foot and bulky dressing in the case of injury to the foot.
14. Walking boot and hinged sole boot—for use where there is injury to the foot but poulticing is not required and horse is to walk gently.
16. Stuffed sausage boot—strapped around coronet it prevents recurrence in the case of capped elbow.
17. Kicking boots—thick felt. For use on mares during service to prevent injury to the stallion if the mare kicks. Replace hobbles.

BANDAGES

General Rules

1. Never draw any one part of the bandage tighter than any other.
2. Do not draw tapes tighter than bandage. May result in swelling and, eventually, a permanent lump on leg. On tail bandage may cause hair to fall out.
3. Tie tapes on outside or inside of leg, never on bone in front or tendon at the back. Fasten in a bow and tuck in spare ends. Never pin.
4. When bandaging uneven surface or swollen legs, use plenty of gamgee or cotton wool and bandage fairly loosely.

Purposes, types, materials and fitting

1. Warmth—Stable bandages.
   (a) Used in stable or travelling.
   (b) Made of flannel or wool.

(c) Seven or eight feet long and four and a half inches wide.

(d) Keep legs warm and encourage circulation.

(e) Fitting—start immediately below knee or hock, continue down leg over fetlock to coronet. Must not be too tight.

2. Support—Exercise Bandages.

(a) Also known as pressure bandages.

(b) Used during work to support back tendons, reinforce weak or strained tendons, or protect leg from injury (thorns, etc.).

(c) Made of crepe or stockinette.

(d) Slightly shorter than Stable Bandages, and two and a half to three inches wide.

(e) Fitting—applied over gamgee or cotton wool with considerable firmness from just below knee to just above fetlock.

  (i) Unroll ten inches and hold obliquely across outside of leg close to knee.

  (ii) Hold roll of bandage close to leg. Take one turn round leg and then allow spare end to fall down outside of leg.

  (iii) Bandage neatly down leg over spare end.

  (iv) At fetlock, turn up remaining inches of spare end and continue to unroll bandage up leg as far as it will go.

  (v) Tie as for stable bandage. For racing, stitch bandage in place.

(f) Do not use bandages unless necessary—soft or tired horse liable to break down.

(g) Adhesive tape, three inches wide, over bandage, helps keep bandage in place in heavy going.

3. Fomenting Bandage—poultices.

(a) Used to help sprains.

(b) Wring out bandage in hot water and apply with two dry bandages on top.

(c) If tendon sheath is torn and leg fills a poultice is more effective than fomenting bandage.

(d) Use Kaolin, Antiphlogistine or Animalintex and prepare according to directions on tin or package.

(e) Poultice should not be applied too hot—should be bearable to back of hand.

(f) Cover poultice with oilcloth to keep in heat.

(g) Bandage securely in place.

(h) Replace poultice every twelve hours until heat is gone from leg.

(i) May also be used on open wound to reduce swelling.

4. Cold Water Bandage.

    (a) Used to reduce heat in leg.

    (b) Made of flannel.

    (c) Steep in cold water and apply to leg. Change frequently or they become hot-water bandages.

    (d) Standing horse in running stream for twenty minutes at a time two or three times a day, or hoseing leg, is more effective.

    (e) Add Epsom salts to cold water to keep bandage cooler.

5. Sweat Bandage.

    (a) Used to reduce swelling or filled legs.

    (b) Steep linen or flannel bandage in hot or cold water and apply to leg. Cover with polythene or oil cloth. Cover with stable bandage.

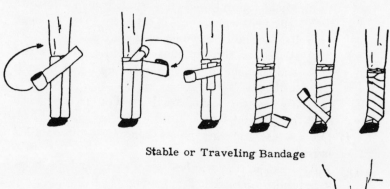

Stable or Traveling Bandage

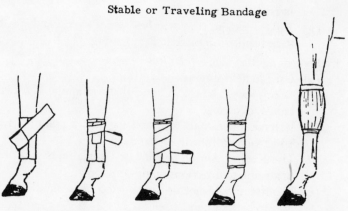

Exercise or Support Bandage   Knee Bandage

78

6. Pressure Bandage—Equihose.
   (a) Used in stable to reduce windgalls and swelling associated with strained tendons.
   (b) Stockinette or crepe bandages over gamgee or cotton wool.
   (c) Object is to apply an even pressure to disburse swelling.
   (d) Equihose—an elasticated sock on same principle as surgical stockings worn by humans. Made in three shapes, for tendons, fetlock and hock. Suitable for work or for wear in stable. Gives firm support while maintaining even tension throughout its length. May also be used to hold dressing or poultice in place.

Removing Bandages
1. Untie tapes and unwind bandage quickly—pass from hand to hand.
2. Never roll bandage when removing.
3. After removing bandage rub tendons and fetlock briskly with palms of hands.
4. Hang up bandages to dry and air.
5. Do not kneel near horse's legs. Bend or crouch to apply bandages.

Tail Bandage.
   (a) Used to protect tail from injury or rubbing during travelling, to improve appearance of tail, and to keep hairs of pulled tail in place.
   (b) Made of stockinette or crepe two and a half to three inches wide.
   (c) Never leave tail bandage on all night.
   (d) Do not apply too tightly and do not tie tapes tighter than bandage or permanent injury to tail hairs may result.
   (e) To apply—damp tail (never bandage as this may cause shrinkage and injury to tail). Place left hand under tail. Unroll six inches and place under tail, holding the end in the left hand. Keep the left hand in place until spare end is secured. After making two turns to secure bandage, make next two turns above to cover hairs at root of tail. Unroll bandage evenly down tail and finish just above end of tail bone. Bend bandaged tail gently back into comfortable position.
   (f) To remove—grasp bandage firmly near root of tail and slide off in a downwards direction.

RUGS—TYPES, MATERIALS, FITTING, CARE

1. Day Rug—woollen, may be bound with braid.
   Purpose—warmth in stable during day.
2. Night Rug—jute, lined with woollen material.
   Purpose—warmth in stable at night.
3. Blankets—woollen.
   Purpose—extra warmth on clipped horse during cold weather.
4. Leather roller—used on all above to keep them in place. Day rugs sometimes provided with rollers to match. Rollers are padded on either side of spine to avoid pressure directly on spine. Breast strap, to prevent roller slipping back, sometimes required.
5. New Zealand Rug—waterproof canvas, partly lined with woollen material.
   Purpose—for use on horse at grass. Not designed for wear in stable. Usually provided with surcingle and legstraps. Afford protection against wind and rain and may be worn as day rugs by stabled horses turned out during daytime.
6. Summer Sheets—cotton, usually provided with "fillet-strings" to prevent sheet blowing up in the wind.
   Purpose—protect groomed horse against dust and flies.
7. Anti-sweat Rugs—open cotton mesh.
   Purpose—used either as sheets or coolers, in summer. May be used under night rug for horse inclined to "break out" after hunting, etc.

Fitting

Correct fitting of night rug, in particular, is very important. All rugs should be fitted so as to avoid pressure on the spine which may cause damage to the back.

(a) Rugs with two attached surcingles most satisfactory. Forward surcingle padded on either side avoids pressure.

(b) Rugs with two surcingles sewn at an angle and crossing under the horse's belly also good.

(c) Separate roller, either leather or web less satisfactory. Rollers must be carefully fitted and kept well stuffed. Breast strap prevents roller slipping back and obviates need to girth up tight.

(d) To prevent rug from rubbing top of neck, forward of withers, stitch a piece of sheepskin to inside of neckpiece.

Care

(a) All clothing should be kept clean, regularly brushed and aired.

(b) All leather parts need regular oiling or soaping. Metal fastenings should be oiled and covered with film of grease.

(c) Summer sheets may be washed but leather parts should

RUGS AND BLANKETS

Roller

Jute Night Rug

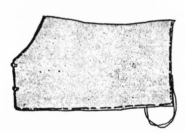

New Zealand Rug

Baker Blanket

be removed first and replaced afterwards.

(d) Winter clothing not required during summer months should first be cleaned, then mended (if necessary), then stored, with moth balls, between sheets of newspaper, until required.

BIBLIOGRAPHY

Saddlery, E. Hartley Edwards, chapters 20 and 21 and pp. 172-175.

The Manual of Horsemanship, B.H.S., pp. 142-149.

First Aid Hints for the Horse Owner, Lyon, p. 137.

Veterinary Notes for Horse Owners, Hayes, pp. 606-611.

CHAPTER 11

CLIPPING AND TRIMMING

NECESSITY FOR CLIPPING

1. To keep condition of a horse through winter months by avoiding heavy sweating.
2. To permit horse to work longer and faster without distress.
3. A clipped horse is easier to get clean and dry and therefore less liable to chills.
4. To save labour in grooming.

Note: Nature provides a layer of fat under the skin after clipping as a protection against cold. The formation of this fat can be assisted by increasing the horse's feed ration for a few days after clipping.

After clipping, adequate clothing must be provided as a substitute for the natural coat.

WHEN TO CLIP

1. First clip usually left till winter coat has set—early October.
2. Coat continues to grow after clipping. Clip as often as necessary, usually every three weeks until Christmas.
3. Do not clip when summer coat is starting to set—clip only once after Christmas, no later than last week of January.

WHERE TO CLIP

1. *Hunters—Full Clip.*
   The whole coat is removed. Usually only done the first time of clipping, after which the Hunter Clip is recommended.
2. *Hunters—Hunter Clip.*
   Legs, as far as elbows and thighs, are left unclipped. Saddle patch is left unclipped. Leaving hair on legs protects them from cold, thorns, mud and cracked heels. Leaving saddle patch prevents back becoming sore or scalded.
3. *Horses being lightly worked—Blanket Clip.*
   Hair is removed from the neck and belly. A blanket shaped patch is left on the body.
4. *Ponies—Trace Clip.*
   Hair is removed from the belly, tops of the legs, and sometimes beneath the neck. Good compromise for ponies living out who must also work and hunt in winter.

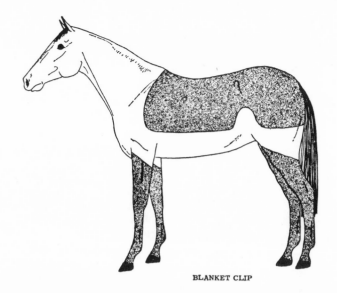

BLANKET CLIP

WHERE NOT TO CLIP

1. *Whiskers.*
   Horse's chief organ of touch. Should be left on except in case of constantly stabled horses, when they may be removed to improve appearance.
2. *Ears.*
   Should never be clipped inside. May be clipped level with the lobes. (The hair inside the ears is a protection from cold and a filter for dirt and bugs.)
3. *Cat Hairs.*
   May be removed by singeing—see below.
4. *Heels and Fetlocks.*
   May be trimmed with scissors and comb if necessary. (Remember, the horse's "feather" is the natural means by which water is prevented from collecting in the heels, and causing cracked heels.)

SINGEING

The removal of long hairs (cat hairs) which appear in various parts of the coat after clipping. A singeing lamp, which gives a small flame, is passed lightly over the body. Lamp must be kept moving in order to avoid burning the horse.

83

MANE PULLING AND TAIL TRIMMING

The Mane

1. *Pulling*
   (a) to thin an over thick mane.
   (b) to shorten a long mane.
   (c) to permit mane to lie flat.

   Method: (i) Pull after exercise or on warm day when pores are open.
   (ii) Remove long hairs from underneath first. Wind a few at a time round comb and pluck briskly out.
   (iii) Never pull the top hair, nor any hairs which stand up after plaiting, as this will form an upright fringe on the crest.
   (iv) Never use scissors or clippers on the mane.

2. *Hogging*
   (a) to eliminate work involved in the care of the mane.
   (b) also used when horse grows ragged mane which spoils appearance.

   Method: (i) Mane is completely removed with clippers.
   (ii) Horse's head should be held low, crest stretched (assistant should stand in front holding ears and gently force head down).
   (iii) Use clippers working from withers towards poll.
   (iv) Hogging needs to be repeated every three to four weeks.
   (v) Once hogged, a mane takes two years to grow out and may never regain its former appearance.

3. *Plaiting*
   (a) to show off neck and crest.
   (b) to train mane to fall on the desired side of the neck.
   (c) for neatness.

   Method: (i) Damp mane with wet water brush.
   (ii) Divide mane into required number of equal parts (always an even number counting forelock).
   (iii) commence plaiting with first section immediately behind ears.

(iv) Three-quarters of the way down the plait take a piece of thread (or wool) at its middle part and join into plait.

(v) When plait is completed, loop ends of thread round plait and pull tight.

(vi) Having completed all plaits (which should be approximately equal in length if mane is properly pulled) pass both ends of thread through the eye of the needle and push needle through plait from underneath, near the crest.

(vii) Remove needle. Bind thread tightly round the plait. Cut off spare ends with scissors.

(viii) Plait may be secured with rubber band instead of thread. Loop the band several times round the end of finished plait. Turn end of plait underneath and loop the band round the whole until secure.

The Tail

1. *Pulling*
   (a) To improve appearance.
   (b) To show off quarters.
   Method: (i) Groom tail well, remove all tangles.
   (ii) Start at the dock, removing all the hair underneath. Then work sideways removing hair evenly on both sides of tail.
   (iii) Remove only a few hairs at a time with a short, sharp pull.
   (iv) Do not pull tails of horses or ponies living out as they need full tails as a protection from the weather.

2. *Banging*
   (a) To show off hocks.
   (b) Prevent tail from becoming straggly.
   (c) To prevent tail collecting mud.
   Method: (i) Assistant places arm beneath root of tail.
   (ii) Cut off end of tail squarely at the level of the points of the hocks.

3. *A Switch Tail*
   Continue pulling to half the length of the tail. Allow the ends of the tail to grow in a natural point.

4. *Plaiting*
   (a) Useful alternative to tail pulling.
   (b) Improves appearance without depriving horse of the
       protection of a full tail.
   Method: (i) Damp tail with wet water brush in dock region.
          (ii) Separate a few hairs on either side of the top of
               the tail and knot together with thread.
         (iii) Separate small bunches of hair on either side
               and plait in with knot which hangs down centre
               of tail.
          (iv) Continue plaiting downwards in this way,
               gathering small bunches from either side, for
               about two-thirds of the length of the dock.
           (v) Continue plaiting centre hairs of the tail only
               to form a free hanging "pigtail".

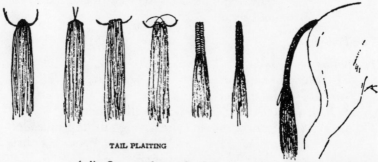

TAIL PLAITING

          (vi) Secure the end of the "pigtail" with thread and
               loop it back under itself to the point where
               side hairs ceased to be included. Stitch loop to-
               gether to form double thickness plait.

5. *Washing*
   (a) To clean tail.
   (b) To improve appearance.
   Method: (i) Groom tail well.
          (ii) Using a bucket of warm water, wet tail and
               shampoo using yellow soap or horse shampoo.
               Use fingers actively.
         (iii) Change the water and rinse tail thoroughly.
          (iv) Squeeze gently with the hands and then swing
               tail to dislodge remaining water.
           (v) Using clean body brush, brush out tail a few
               hairs at a time.

(vi) Bandage with clean dry tail bandage.

Note: Regular bandaging, after grooming, helps to keep pulled tail in good shape. Do not leave bandage on all night. To protect plaited tail during journey, bandage carefully. Remove bandage by unwinding gently, not by pulling off in the usual way.

POINTS TO NOTE WHEN CLIPPING

1. Ensure that horse is dry and well groomed.
2. If possible, clip by daylight. Clipping box must be well lighted.
3. Allow horse to become accustomed to the sound of the clippers before actually using them.
4. Before starting, use soap or chalk to mark the legs and saddle patch. (Saddle the horse and mark under the flap.)
5. Do not push or force clippers. The weight of the clipping head provides all the pressure needed.
6. Clip against the coat. Take as much with one sweep as possible.
7. Leave difficult bits to the last.
8. It is useless to continue clipping if horse breaks out.
9. Application of a twitch may have the effect of making horse sweat. Do not use one unless absolutely necessary.
10. If clippers get hot stop clipping and switch them off. Continue when they are cool again. Hot clippers will make the horse restless.

CARE AND USE OF CLIPPERS

1. Clippers must always be earthed, either with a three-point plug or by fastening a wire from clipper head to a drainpipe leading to the ground.
2. Arrange all wires so that horse cannot step on them.
3. Keep clippers clean and well oiled. Blades may be run in kerosene for cleaning but must be dried and oiled afterwards to prevent rusting.
4. Clean and oil frequently during operation.
5. The tension of the blades should be just sufficient to clip. New blades can be slackened off after they have started to clip.
6. Keep a spare set of sharpened blades to hand.
7. Never clip with dull blades—get them sharpened regularly.

8. When not in use keep clippers, clean and oiled, in a safe, dry place. Blades and head break very easily if machine is dropped or knocked from shelf, etc.

TYPES OF CLIPPING MACHINE

1. *Hand Clippers:* Slow and laborious. Useful for clipping whiskers, etc.

2. *Hand operated wheel machine clippers:* Old-fashioned but useful with nervous horse as they are quiet. Whole-time assistant necessary to turn handle.

3. *Electric Clippers:*

    Motor and Clipping head in one: The motor is held in the hand.

    Advantage: Easy to handle, portable.

    Disadvantage: Inclined to overheat and get clogged with hairs.

    Hanging Machine: Has a strong motor and is the best machine if a large number of horses are to be clipped.

    Advantage: No overheating.

    Disadvantage: Must be hung from very strong beam. Cable from machine to clipper head is heavy and awkward to manœuvre and the lead is too short to follow a fidgety horse around the stable.

    Machine on Operator's Back.

    Advantage: Good motor and good manœuvrability.

    Disadvantage: Rather heavy. Cable a little difficult to handle.

4. *Vacuum Clippers:* As used in cowsheds. Clippers are connected to a suction plant.

    Advantage: Cannot break down as no machine involved. Can only be interrupted by failure in power supply. Very quiet.

    Disadvantage: Not very powerful. Would not clip a very heavy coat.

Note: All the machines described are made by various manufacturers. The best and most well-known are: Wolesley, Cooper-Stewart (Stewart Clipmaster), and Lister.

BIBLIOGRAPHY

The Manual of Horsemanship, B.H.S., pp. 168-179.
First Aid Hints for the Horse Owner, Lyon, pp. 21-22 and 26-27.

CHAPTER 12

VICES AND REMEDIES

KICKING IN THE BOX

Causes:
1. Boredom—horse likes to hear the noise.
2. Idleness.
3. Irritability.
4. Rats and mice.
5. Parasites.

Remedies:
1. Pad box or stall with bales of straw or matting.
2. Line box with gorse (effective for horse who paws or kicks at door with front feet).
3. Hang a sack of straw behind hindquarters.
4. Put hobbles on horse and attach to the headcollar by ropes.
5. If possible turn horse out to grass for six months —he may forget and overcome habit.
6. Keep horse well exercised. Divide exercise into two periods daily instead of one.

STAMPING AND PAWING

Causes:
1. Same as for kicking, and also
2. Lack of bedding.
3. Impatience, etc.
4. Sign of internal pain or colic.

Remedies:
1. Removal of cause.
2. Good deep clean bed.
3. Some of the remedies for kicking will also help with pawing horses.

BITING AND SNAPPING

Causes:
1. Mismanagement.
2. Irritation of horse by improper grooming.
3. Feeding of tit bits.
4. Failure to stop playful snapping in early stages— it soon becomes a serious vice.

Remedies: 1. Firmness and kindness. Sharp slap on side of muzzle at the crucial moment will usually effect a cure in early stages.

2. Tie up confirmed biters before grooming, to protect groom.

3. Groom carefully and with consideration. Some horses are more ticklish than others. Avoid irritating horse by rough or careless grooming.

CRIB BITING AND WIND SUCKING

Serious vices which constitute unsoundness. Crib biters take hold of projecting object with their teeth and swallow air. Causes damage to incisor teeth and may result in inability to graze properly. Wind suckers arch neck and swallow air, usually without biting on to anything. Swallowing air into the stomach is a common cause of flatulance and colic. Impairs digestion, often prevents horse putting on flesh.

Causes: 1. Idleness.

2. Lack of bulk food.

3. Irritation of the stomach which causes a specific craving.

4. Horse may start cribbing by gnawing at manger when being groomed or by gnawing unseasoned wood.

Remedies: 1. Prevent boredom—divide exercise into two periods daily.

2. Paint woodwork in box or stall with bitter aloes or other anti-chew mixture.

3. If possible, keep horse in loose box, not tied up.

4. Have rock salt constantly available.

5. Give horse plenty of bulk food. Keep an unlimited supply of fresh, clean water constantly available to him.

6. A broad strap fastened round the thin part of the neck tightly enough to prevent the muscles contracting will help to check wind sucking.

7. Isolate horses which crib bite or wind suck as other horses are liable to copy them.

WEAVING

A continuous rocking or swaying action of the forelegs followed by a similar action of the head. Weavers cannot rest and deteriorate in condition.

Bad cases may become lame. Starts as a habit, develops into a vice and eventually becomes a nervous disease. A horse which weaves cannot be warranted sound.

Causes: 1. Boredom.
          2. Nervousness — horse may be an intermittent weaver, only actually weaving when someone is in the stable.

Remedies: 1. Remove cause, where possible. In case of boredom, apply same remedies as for crib biting.
          2. Provide well bedded loose box. Encourage horse to lie down.
          3. Two bricks, or tyres, suspended over the half door so that the horse knocks into them first one side, then the other, as he weaves are sometimes effective.
          4. Avoid periods of idleness—or turn horse out to pasture rather than letting him stand in the box.
          5. Isolate horses which weave as other horses will imitate the habit.

REFUSAL TO LIE DOWN

Some horses suffer no apparent harm from refusing to lie down, but legs suffer and will last longer if rested.

Causes: 1. Nervousness—strange surroundings, or horse may have been cast.
          2. Lack of bedding.
          3. If horse is in a stall, shank may be too short.

Remedies: 1. Put horse in loose box with deep, clean bed. Try different forms of bedding.
          2. Give long, steady work for two or three days.
          3. Bring horse in late at night (if he is tired and can once be persuaded to lie down, he may overcome his nervousness).

EATING BEDDING AND DROPPINGS

A sign of depraved appetite.

Causes: 1. Boredom.
          2. Lack of bulk food.
          3. Lack of mineral salts.
          4. Worm infestation.

Remedies: 1. Removal of cause.
          2. Bed on peat moss. Mix new and used bedding well.

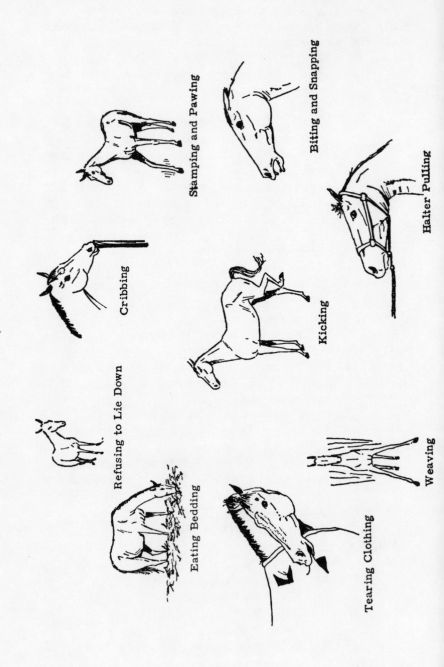

Stamping and Pawing

Biting and Snapping

Halter Pulling

Cribbing

Kicking

Refusing to Lie Down

Eating Bedding

Weaving

Tearing Clothing

3. Sprinkle bedding with Lysol.
4. Horses may have to wear a cradle, or a muzzle.
5. Tie horse up before exercise so he cannot reach bedding or droppings.

TEARING CLOTHING AND BANDAGES

Causes: 1. Horse may be trying to alleviate itching associated with a skin disease.
2. Idleness.

Remedies: 1. Examine and treat for skin disease any particular spot horse bites.
2. Paint clothing with some nasty tasting liquid.
3. Use leather bib hanging from back of head stall, behind lower lip. Or use muzzle.
4. Keep plenty of bulk food and salt available.

HALTER PULLING

Causes: 1. Fear. Young horse may pull back, feel the halter tighten around muzzle, become frightened and struggle harder and eventually get free.
2. Past experience that he can free himself this way.
3. Horse kept tied in stall may start halter pulling if there is too much slope on the floor. His forelegs are higher than his hind legs and he cannot rest, so he pulls back to alter position and forms the habit.
4. Horse kept tied in stall may start halter pulling in order to reach his neighbour in adjoining stall.

Remedies: 1. Prevention is better than cure. Never tie a young horse and leave it unattended.
2. An additional rope round the horse's neck, provided it is carefully secured so that it cannot tighten, will often help.
3. Use an elastic tie rope.
4. For horse tied in stall, fix a rope across back of stall to come in contact with hindquarters if horse pulls back.

BIBLIOGRAPHY

First Aid Hints for the Horse Owner, W. E. Lyon, pp. 147-8.
Horsemen's Veterinary Adviser, Joseph B. Davidson, p. 232.
Veterinary Notes for Horse Owners, M. Horace Hayes, pp. 146-9 and 501-2.
Summerhay's Encyclopædia for Horsemen, pp. 30, 81, 197, 363 and 369.

CHAPTER 13
HEALTH INDICATORS

SIGNS OF GOOD HEALTH

1. Horse alert, head up, ears pricked (back and forwards).
2. Eyes bright. Mucous membrane of the eye salmon pink.
3. Skin supple and loose, coat bright.
4. Droppings should be regular and break on hitting the ground. (Horse passes eight or nine droppings a day which should be greenish or golden in colour, depending on the feed.)
5. Body should be well furnished.
6. Temperature 100° to 101°F. (38°C.).
7. Pulse 36-42 beats per minute.
8. Respiration 8-15 per minute.

HOW TO TAKE A HORSE'S PULSE

Usually taken where facial artery passes under the jaw on either side. May also be taken at median artery, inside foreleg, level with elbow, or on the supra-orbital artery just above and behind the eye. Pulse should be 36 to 42 beats per minute. Pulse can be felt on the following arteries:

1. Facial artery (jaw).
2. Supra-orbital artery (eye).
3. Carotid artery (neck—near jugular vein).
4. Median artery (elbow).

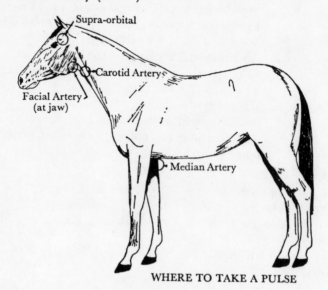

WHERE TO TAKE A PULSE

HOW TO TAKE A HORSE'S TEMPERATURE

Taken in the rectum. Grease thermometer with Vaseline. Gently raise dock and insert thermometer with rotating action. Leave in position for at least the stated time. Withdraw and read.

Normal temperature of a horse is 100°F. (38°C.) and of a foal from 100° to 101·5°. A rise over 102° is abnormal and a temperature of 104° or 105° may indicate serious disease. Call veterinary surgeon.

HOW TO TAKE A HORSE'S RESPIRATION

Watch flanks from behind. Breathing should be even at rate of 8 to 15 per minute.

To test horse for soundness of wind
1. Have horse trotted and cantered in small circle.
2. As horse comes close, listen carefully for any noise as he inhales.
3. Have horse galloped then watch flanks.
4. If horse appears to heave twice on exhalation he has broken wind (over-distention and breakdown of air vesicles of lungs).
5. No cure for broken wind. In early stages all food should be damp. Mix linseed oil in feed two or three times weekly. Horse may be kept workably sound for some time.
6. Broken wind is not considered hereditary.

A HORSE IN GOOD CONDITION

When horse is physically fit and able to undertake, without strain, the work which he may be required to perform, he is said to be in good condition.
1. Conditioning is a gradual process.
2. Depends on: (a) Good feeding.
   (b) Good exercise.
   (c) Good stable management. (Strapping and wisping).
   (d) Attention to detail.

Good Feeding
1. Feed only first quality forage, best oats and old hay.
2. Feed little and often.
3. Feed at a regular time.

4. Horses brought up from grass should be fed damp bran and hay only for first week or so. Change from grass to dry food is likely to cause indigestion and coughing.
5. Increase quantity of oats in accordance with increased exercise, as horse gets fitter.
6. Make no sudden changes of diet.

Good Exercise

1. Start with walking exercise. Build up quickly to forty minutes a day.
2. Walking and slow trotting should continue for as long as possible. After fourteen days exercise should be one to one-and-a-half hours daily.
3. Steady trotting uphill excellent for muscling quarters and improving wind.
4. Gradually increase grain from about 8-10 lb. with above exercise, to 10-14 lb. when horse is in hard work (hunting, etc.).
5. Fat acquired at grass is replaced by muscle with long slow exercise. Do not canter or gallop when horse is fat (fast work is liable to affect wind and damage legs).
6. Horse brought up from grass in August will be ready for slow cantering in early October and should have a gallop or two before the end of October, in preparation for hunting.

Good Stable Management

1. Clip as soon as possible. From end of September until end of November clip every three weeks, then once a month. Clip only once after Christmas.
2. Keep horse well clothed—wool blanket under rug.
3. Keep stable well ventilated, but close top half of door at night if very cold.
4. Thorough grooming every day essential to good health.
5. When hunting hard horse needs little exercise. Three-quarters of an hour to stretch the legs on day after hunting, one to one-and-a-half hours on other days.

BIBLIOGRAPHY

First Aid Hints for the Horse Owner, Lyon, pp. 13-22, 112 and 140.
Manual of Horsemanship, B.H.S.

CHAPTER 14

SICK NURSING

GENERAL RULES OF NURSING

1. Good nursing is of primary importance in treatment of disease.
2. 'Good nursing' implies intelligent appreciation of the minute wants and needs of the patient; and kind, prompt attention to these needs.
3. Quiet is. essential. Place patient in roomy, well ventilated loose box, away from bustle of yard if possible. Do not confuse ventilation with draughts.
4. Bed down with plenty of short straw. (Ensures freedom of movement.)
5. Loose box should have low half-door so patient can lean head over. Especially useful in diseases of the respiratory passages.
6. In cases of infection of the eye and nervous system, the loose box should be darkened as much as possible.
7. Even in cases of wounds where horse must be tied up, loose box is preferable to a stall—fresh air will circulate better.
8. Keep patient warm with light woollen clothing. In some areas, on some occasions, when the weather is very cold, the judicious use of artificial heating of the stable may be permitted. Sick horses cannot carry heavy clothing without fatigue, nor keep up body temperature by food. Never use artificial heating at the expense of ventilation.
9. Keep loose box clean, dry and sweet. Use powder disinfectant to help keep floor dry.
10. Carry out all medication, fomentation, application of dressings, syringing, etc., with great care, at appropriate times as instructed by veterinary surgeon.
11. Avoid noise and bright lights during night visits to the patient.
12. If horse is very sick, do not leave him alone. He will derive comfort from presence of a sympathetic person. Also wise to have attendant on hand in case of crisis.

97

WARMTH

1. Maintain warmth by light, woollen clothing. Bandage legs loosely for additional warmth. Do not put heavy clothing on very weak horse.
2. Warmth may be restored to the body by gentle rubbing with the hands—especially to the legs of the horse.
3. To discover if horse is cold—feel his ears, if they are cold the whole horse is cold. He may also shiver.
4. Clothing should be put on loosely. Loose clothing is easier to wear and warmer than tight clothing.
5. Remove clothing gradually, shake and brush it twice daily. Never have horse completely stripped.
6. If circulation is poor, use a hood for added warmth.

WATERING

1. Unless instructed to the contrary by the veterinary surgeon, keep a bucket of fresh water at a convenient height, constantly in the box.
2. Change water frequently. Even if horse doesn't drink, he will wash his mouth out periodically. In diseases with nasal discharge the frequent changing of the water is even more important.

FEEDING

1. Maintain horse's strength as much as possible by tempting him with small quantities of food at frequent intervals.
2. Food must be suitable for requirements of case.
3. Do not try to force horse to eat.
4. The state of the appetite is a good guide to whether the system requires food or not. When temperature is high, horse is unlikely to eat.
5. Skimmed milk, diluted with water at first, will be taken by most horses.
6. As recovery starts, tempt horse by hand feeding small quantities of a variety of foods, e.g., green grass, green oats, lucerne, carrots, apples, linseed and bran mash, boiled barley, gruel, linseed tea, hay tea, milk and eggs, etc.
7. Do not leave food in manger if refused by horse. Leaving it even a short while will dull the appetite.
8. *Note.* The foods listed above are all laxative. A most essential factor in restoring condition to a sick animal is the provision of laxative feed.

SALT

Should always be present in some form in the loose box.

GROOMING

Whether to groom will depend on degree of illness. Consult the veterinary surgeon. Hand rubbing is beneficial. If horse is well enough, groom gently, taking care to keep him out of draughts. Do not strip him completely but rather 'quarter' him.

EXERCISE

1. Start gradually after all dangers of relapse have passed.
2. Do not start exercise without the authority of the veterinary surgeon.
3. First day—walk across yard and back.
4. Second day—lead out for five to ten minutes. Gradually increase exercise by a few minutes each day.

BANDAGES (Hot fomentations, Cold water bandages)

1. Renew hot or cold water bandages every half hour.
2. Temperature of hot bandage should be no hotter than the hand can bear.
3. Apply above affected part and allow water to trickle down.
4. After application, cover area to avoid chill.
5. Legs may also be cold bathed by hosing, standing in a stream or bucket.

REMOVAL OF SHOES

If horse is obviously to be laid up for a long time, have shoes removed.

DISCHARGE FROM NOSTRILS

1. Encourage discharge by feeding from the ground.
2. Small quantity of Vick Vapour Rub may be placed in outside nostril.
3. Steaming is beneficial. Place handful of hay in nosebag or corner of a sack; add one tablespoon Friar's Balsam, Menthol or Oil of Eucalyptus; pour on a kettleful of boiling water. Hold mouth of sack or nosebag over horse's nostrils.

DISINFECTING AFTER CONTAGIOUS DISEASE

1. Scrub stable walls, manger, etc., thoroughly with either: solution made up of two handfuls washing soda to one bucket hot water, or one tablespoonful Lysol to one pint water.

2. Wear rubber gloves and scrub thoroughly to remove all dirt and dust.

3. Spray with strong disinfectant to kill all germs.

4. Limewash stable with mixture of one bucket of Limewash and one pint Carbolic acid.

USEFUL MEDICAL SUPPLIES

General

Veterinary clinical thermometer.
Blunt-pointed surgical scissors.
Bandages—2in. and 3in.
Several small rolls cotton wool.
Roll Gamgee tissue.
Some 1 oz. packets Lint.
Oiled silk.
Bottle Veterinary Embrocation.
Bottle of Witch Hazel lotion.
Jar of common salt.
Packet of Epsom salts.
Bottle of glycerine.
1 lb. tin Kaolin Paste.

ADDITIONAL USEFUL ITEMS

For   *Have*

Abrasions: Gentian violet, lanolin, Antiseptic Veterinary Ointment, White Vaseline.

Antiseptics: *Liquid:* Iodine, Hydrogen Peroxide (mix ½ pint Peroxide with 5 pints water).
               Soap: Septisol (mild).
               Powder: Sulphanilamide, Boric Powder, other antibiotic powder recommended by Veterinary Surgeon.

Colic:	Colic drink made up by Veterinary Surgeon. Or, drink made up of 2 oz. Bicarbonate of Soda, (Baking Powder) and 2 oz. Ground Ginger in 1 pint warm water. Or, 2 tablespoons turpentine, 1½ pints linseed oil, and 2 tablespoons whisky or brandy.
Coughs:	Cough Electuary, Vick's Vapour Rub.
Cracked Heels (Scratches):	Lanolin. Fungicidal Ointment.
Cuts:	See Abrasions.
Eyes:	Boracic Lotion, Boracic Ointment, Collyrium.
Fungus:	Medicated Shampoo.
Girth Galls:	Gall Remedy—see Abrasions.
Hooves:	Cornucrescine, Hooflex, or Hoof dressing made up of equal parts Pine Tar and Vegetable Oil. Feed Corn Oil (1 tablespoon daily) for flakey hooves.
Leg Cooling or Reducing:	Fuller's Earth, Antiphlogistine, Animalintex, Amoricaine Powder.
Poultice:	Antiphlogistine, Animalintex, Epsom Salts.
Proud Flesh:	Caustic dressing, caustic dusting powder made up of 3 parts Boracic Powder, one part copper sulphate, may be applied daily.
Sore Backs:	Antiseptic Veterinary Packs, Lead lotion, Rubbing Alcohol (to harden).
Strains:	White Liniment, Antiphlogistine, Deep Liniment, Bigeloil, Animalintex.
Worms:	Equizole, Equiguard, or remedy supplied by Veterinary Surgeon.
Thrush:	Coppertox, or remedy supplied by Veterinary Surgeon.

BIBLIOGRAPHY

First Aid Hints for the Horse Owner, Lt.-Col. W. E. Lyon, Collins, Third Edition, 1951

CHAPTER 15

PREPARATION FOR AND TRANSPORTATION OF HORSES

TRANSPORTATION BY AIR

1. This method now used almost exclusively for Racehorses travelling long distances, also for teams of horses attending international events.
2. Air transport far superior to travel by sea. Journeys take only hours instead of days; horses suffer no loss of condition.
3. Cost is high but transport companies now liaise with air charter firms and horses shipped in a full load cost much less.
4. Horses usually tranquilized for travel by air but the advice of the veterinary surgeon should be taken on this subject.

TRANSPORTATION BY SEA

1. Very slow compared to transportation by air.
2. Cost is the same whether one horse is shipped or twenty.
3. Nearly all horses suffer loss of body weight and condition.
4. Horses often subject to coughs and virus attacks during shipping, or upon arrival at their destination.
5. Horses suffer considerable discomfort during rough crossings.

TRANSPORTATION BY RAIL

1. Still possible in some areas, but now generally superseded by road transport.
2. Railway companies do not provide an attendant to travel with horses—shipper must provide groom if required.
3. Horse box may be shunted into siding and forgotten for several days.

TRANSPORTATION BY ROAD

1. Best way to transport horses overland, even for quite long journeys.
2. Preparations must be made in advance for over-night stops during long journeys.
3. In the U.S. a Veterinary certificate is required for inter-State travel.

Trailers
(a) Most common form of overland transportation.
(b) Usually cheapest way of moving from one to four horses.
(c) Most trailers are too small in height and width to accommodate horse comfortably.
(d) Too few drivers of cars really know how to start, stop, turn or back with a horse and trailer.
(e) Car and trailer is often quite a dangerous combination.
(f) Many horses are soured for travel following bad experiences loading, unloading or in transit in trailers.
(g) It is essential to check condition of hitch, brakes, lights, connections and floor of trailer regularly.

Motor horsebox or van
(a) By far the best method of overland transport for horses.
(b) Horse has plenty of head room (most important for young and nervous animals).
(c) Plenty of light and room inside the van.
(d) Animal is not subjected to the buffeting around often experienced in a trailer.
(e) Many nervous horses who will not travel in trailers are perfectly happy in horsebox.

PRELIMINARY PREPARATIONS FOR ANY JOURNEY

1. Check horse for soundness. See that shoes are in good condition.
2. Veterinary examination is advisable to ensure that no contagious disease is present—especially if horse is to be sold. In U.S. a Veterinary Certificate is required at some inter-State borders and also at Mexican and Canadian borders.
3. Notify person receiving horse of approximate time of arrival.
4. Prepare equipment required at destination (if travelling to a show or competition).
5. Even for short journeys, e.g., one day show, take bucket and water in water carrier.
6. If journey is to be long, prepare sufficient hay and feed for entire journey.

ACTUAL PREPARATIONS ON DAY OF DEPARTURE

1. Clothing will depend on climate, time of year, etc. Cotton sheet, with fillet strings, may be all that is required. Take rugs, whether worn or not, for use during journey or on return from show, in case they are required.

2. Put on stable bandages, with plenty of cotton wool or gamgee; or shipping boots.
3. Over-reach boots on front feet are an added precaution.
4. Knee boots and hock boots are advisable, particularly on long journeys.
5. A tail guard will prevent injury to the tail or unsightly rubbing. For short journeys put on a crepe tail bandage under the tail guard. Do not tie bandage too tightly.
6. Leather headcollar should be worn in preference to rope

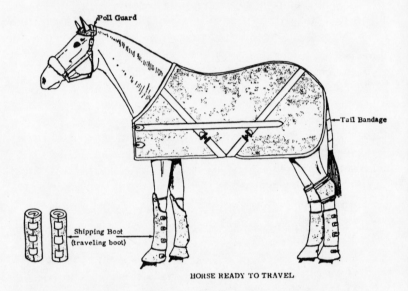

Poll Guard

Tail Bandage

Shipping Boot
(traveling boot)

HORSE READY TO TRAVEL

halter. Should be strong, well fitting, with slightly longer than normal headrope. If journey is long, pad headcollar with sheepskin where it may rub.

7 If horse is head shy or nervous use a poll guard (American, 'head bumper').

LOADING

1. If horse is accustomed to travelling, lead quietly up ramp, secure to ring or bar with normal length of rope, using a quick release knot, and tie up a net of hay within easy reach.
2. If horse is difficult to load try:
   (a) loading stable companion first and follow up the ramp close on his heels.

(b) tempting a shy loader with oats. In any case, shy loader should be rewarded with oats as soon as he is in the box and he should continue to be rewarded every time he is loaded until all his fear has been overcome.

(c) Using two lunge lines, attach one to each side of ramp rail, or on any convenient portion of entrance. Leave lunge reins stretched out on ground with one person ready to take hold of the end of each rein. Lead horse up to ramp quietly and stand him straight. Helpers now pick up lunge reins and walk quietly towards each other and pass each other, so that reins cross over and rest on the horse just above the hocks. Helpers gradually but firmly pull the reins or ropes from the sides so that they tighten behind the horse as he is led forward up the ramp.

(d) Load really difficult horses wearing a snaffle bridle as well as a leather headcollar. This gives handler much more control in case of horse attempting to rear, run away, etc.

3. When loading horses, everyone present, except the one leading the horse, should stand well behind the line of the ramp and the horse's quarters. Standing in front of the horse's eye is enough to stop even a willing loader and will certainly stop a shy one.

4. Most carriers owning and operating horse boxes are experienced in loading difficult horses and the task may often be safely left to them.

5. During long journeys, arrangements must be made for watering and feeding of horses en route.

6. On journeys taking several days, where overnight stops are not planned, some provision must be made for exercising during short stops. Horses should also be closely watched as some will not urinate in a horse box. Retention of urine can lead very quickly to serious health problems.

INSURANCE

1. Special insurance policies are available for the show season, or for short periods of time, to cover horses against show and transportation risks.

2. Most carriers with horse boxes for hire have policies which fully cover any animal against transit risks in their vehicles.

CHAPTER 16

CARE OF THE HUNTER

THE DAY BEFORE HUNTING
1. Give horse normal exercise for one-and-a-half hours.
2. Satisfy yourself that horse is sound. If in doubt, don't hunt. Heat normally comes to a leg before a sprain.
3. Check feet and shoes.
4. Check tack—stitching on stirrup leathers and reins, buckles on girths, etc.
5. Give an extra feed about 8.0 p.m.

THE MORNING OF THE HUNT
1. Feed early—three to four hours before you plan to leave.
2. Muck out and groom in normal way. Try to avoid exciting horse by change of routine or he may not eat.
3. Leave plaiting of mane and tail until horse has finished eating.
4. If a stranger to the district, check the hunting map of the

READY TO GO TO THE HUNT

area so that you can follow bridlepaths to the meet. (Meets marked in red.) Always go to the meet, do not go direct to the covert.

THINGS TO TAKE WITH YOU

1. Money.
2. Piece of string.
3. Clean handkerchief.
4. Folding hoof pick.
5. Pocket knife.
6. Antiseptic cream.
7. Wire cutters.

AT THE MEET

1. If hacking, do not hurry. Arrive at meet with horse cool and quiet.
2. Dismount and slacken girth. Walk horse around. Lead him on the grass and allow him to stale.
3. Tighten girth and mount. Keep horse on the move if it is a cold day.
4. If travelling to meet by horsebox or trailer, take horse out, tack up and walk and trot about for twenty minutes to loosen him up.
5. Before hounds move off, check girth.

DURING THE DAY

1. Save your horse in the morning. Don't jump unnecessarily so that horse will still be fresh in the afternoon.
2. Always ride with judgment and spare horse when possible.
3. At check, dismount, slacken girth, turn horse's head into wind to help him get his 'second wind'.
4. In plough, ride down a furrow. Try to stay on downwind side of hounds—it is easier to hear hounds and they are more likely to turn downwind.
5. Jumping into plough, go slowly—heavy landing may cause over-reach.
6. Ride fence with ditch on take-off side slowly and fence with ditch on landing side faster, to give horse chance to get more spread.
7. Jumping timber, gates, walls or any solid fixed fence, check horse well forty yards away, then present him to the fence.

8. Never jump on the heels of the horse ahead of you. Riding too close may cause fatal accident if the horse and rider in front fall.
9. Save your horse going uphill. Set steady pace, using good judgment coming downhill.
10. When the horse has had enough, go home.

ON THE WAY HOME

1. If going by horsebox or trailer, walk and jog alternately back to vehicle so that horse arrives there cool. Do not load a hot and sweat horse as he will catch a chill.
2. If hacking, walk and trot alternately. Bring horse home dry, cool and as quickly as is reasonably possible.
3. If horse is very tired, walk and lead him the last mile or so with loosened girth. This will help to prevent sore back by allowing circulation to be restored gradually.
4. It is inadvisable to give horse a long drink on the way home. Allow him one or two mouthfuls during hack home or before loading into horsebox or trailer.

ON ARRIVAL AT THE STABLE

1. Do not remove the saddle if the horse's back is hot and sweating. Loosen girth and wait until he is dry to remove saddle.
2. On arriving at the stable, give horse a drink of water which has had the chill taken off. After an hour or so he can have more water.
3. Loose box should be well bedded down ready and hay net hung up before horse returns. Remove bridle. Throw rugs over horse (inside out if he is still damp), and encourage him to stale by whistling and shaking up the straw.
4. If legs are wet and muddy, put on woollen stable bandages over straw, quite loosely. Leave horse to have a mouthful of hay.
5. Return in quarter of an hour or so to remove saddle. Wisp the back to restore circulation and keep it warm. Ensure all vital parts are dry, if not, dry especially the loins and throat area to prevent horse catching cold.
6. Check horse's ears, they should be warm and dry. If not, rub gently until they are.
7. Feed bran mash.

8. When horse has eaten, start to clean him. Only clean the worst off, leave final grooming until morning. The horse is tired and should be left to rest as soon as possible.
9. Remove bandages from legs which should be dry by then. Brush legs, removing dry mud and checking for cuts and thorns (treat any cuts or thorn injuries found).
10. If horse is cool and dry, showing no sign of breaking out, put on night rugs. After he has been in for two hours, refill water bucket and give grain feed. If he is exhausted, feed boiled oats as they are easier to digest.
11. If it is cold, or horse is exhausted, replace stable bandages (preferably over cotton wool) for added warmth and comfort.
12. Visit horse every hour until he is quite dry. Make sure he has plenty of hay.
13. In clay country, oil horse's belly and inside of thighs lightly with olive oil, neatsfoot oil or liquid paraffin before hunting to prevent clay from clinging. Use Vaseline in heels to prevent cracked heels.

TACK

1. Clean tack that night if possible.
2. Wash thoroughly to remove all mud and sweat. Dry with chamois. Then soap thoroughly.

THE FOLLOWING MORNING

1. Undo breast strap of rug, remove bandages. Trot horse out to discover any sign of weakness or lameness.
2. Continue normal stable routine. Check horse carefully during grooming for any cuts or thorns overlooked the night before.
3. Exercise should consist of leading out, at walk (in rug if weather is cold) for half an hour or so.
4. A hunter brought home by 3.00 p.m. should be fit to hunt one to two days afterwards. If brought home by 5.00 p.m. he should be fit to hunt four or five days afterwards. If brought in by 7.00 p.m. he should be fit to hunt once a week.

BIBLIOGRAPHY

The Manual of Horsemanship, B.H.S.
Riding, Mrs. V. D. S. Williams, pp. 88-92.
Riding to Hounds in America, William P. Wadsworth, M.F.H.

CHAPTER 17

ROUGHING OFF AND TURNING OUT

GENERAL CONSIDERATIONS

1. Object of turning out—to give horse a complete rest and an opportunity to put on flesh after a hard season's hunting.
2. Before horse is turned out he must be 'roughed off'—i.e., prepared gradually, usually about fourteen days is sufficient.

ROUGHING OFF

1. Remove one blanket or rug.
2. If top half of the door has been closed, leave open all the time.
3. Gradually reduce the amount of grain fed and increase the amount of hay. When horse begins to feel grain reduction, reduce exercise.
4. Stop thorough grooming. Simply remove stable stains, mud and sweat with dandy brush. Leave the natural grease in the coat as protection against the weather.
5. After a week or ten days, remove the second rug.
6. If possible, turn horse out in small paddock for an hour or so each day (in New Zealand rug at first, if necessary) to accustom him to being out. All horses when first turned out will gallop and play. If paddock is small and safely fenced risk of injury is reduced.
7. When horse is roughed off, choose a mild day to turn out completely. Turn out early in the day and check horse at least once during the afternoon. If all is well, leave him out all night. Check again next morning.

TIME OF YEAR TO TURN HORSES OUT

Will depend on climate. In England it is not advisable to turn out thoroughbreds, and leave out at night, until first or second week of May.

In valley countries the hunting season usually finishes early due to damage that may be done to crops. Rough off early (to save expense) and turn horse out during the day in New Zealand rug. Continue to bring in at night until weather is suitable to turn horse out completely.

FEET

1. If horse has good feet and is being turned on to good land shoes may be removed and feet rasped, to prevent horn from splitting, before turning out.
2. If feet are hard and brittle, keep front shoes on and remove hind shoes only.
3. Alternatively, remove hind shoes and shoe front feet with 'grass tips'. Tips must taper off well to the back, keeping frog in contact with the ground.
4. Horses out to grass need their feet trimming once a month. Grass tips must be removed each month and replaced, otherwise toe will get too long and heel too low, causing pressure on the tendons.

LEGS

1. Bony enlargements, sprained tendons, etc., should be blistered before turning horse out.
2. Blistering should be done before fly time. Flies may cause the sore to go septic.

TEETH

Examine teeth for sharp edges. Have floated (rasped) if necessary.

CHOICE OF FIELD

1. Choose field where horse has good range rather than small field. In a dry summer, a horse on a good range will come in hard. In a wet summer, if horse is in a small field, he will come in soft and fat.
2. Good safe fences are essential. Post and rail is best. Ensure that fences are free of loose strands of wire.
3. Ensure that field is free from unnecessary hazards—e.g., pieces of farm machinery which may become half hidden in grass, broken bottles, etc.
4. There must be a plentiful supply of fresh water in the field. Running stream is ideal if sufficiently deep. Automatically filled water tank is also good. Ponds are not generally good —usually stagnant. (In clay country a pond has one advantage, horses stand and walk in the pond and the clay acts as a mild blister.)

5. Horses are gregarious and should not be turned out alone. An old pony makes an ideal companion for a valuable thoroughbred—or when weaning a youngster.

6. Before turning horse out, feed some green fodder, lucerne, etc., to accustom stomach gradually to green food. If turning horse into fairly lush pasture, feed him before turning out so that he will be less inclined to overeat on grass. If turning horse on to less good grazing, turn him out hungry so that he will be less inclined to gallop about.

7. The field should have good shade trees and at least one spot where horse can shelter from wind and rain in the event of summer storms, e.g., good thick hedge on windward side.

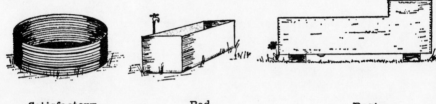

Satisfactory
But Inconvenient

Bad
Sharp Edges
Projecting Tap

Best
Self-Filling With
Ball-cock Enclosed

METHODS OF WATERING HORSES AT GRASS

CARE OF HORSES AT GRASS

1. Visit horses turned out to grass at least once a day.

2. Check for injuries, and lameness.

3. Check fences and water supply periodically.

4. In the heat of summer, when flies are bad, bring horses into the stable during the day and leave with fresh water and small quantity of hay. Turn out at night.

5. Grass is at its best in May and June and horse will not need grain. By the end of July the grass deteriorates and horses still out should be given a small grain feed daily.

BRINGING HORSE UP FROM GRASS

1. Hunters should be brought in in August.
2. Feed small grain feed daily for last few weeks at grass.
3. It takes approximately six weeks to get horses fit for hunting. If left out too long horses come in soft, without muscle, and if hunted too soon will lose fat without forming muscle and get poor.
4. Bringing horses in, there are three main considerations to keep in mind.

   (a) Prevention of coughs, colds and sore throats.
      (i) Plenty of fresh air essential. Leave top half of door open.
      (ii) Horse must not be made to sweat during first week in stable.
      (iii) Feed hay well damped. Feed only small quantity of grain mixed with chaff and damp bran.
      (iv) Plenty of walking exercise is essential. As horse becomes fit, slow trotting uphill is an excellent muscling exercise.

   (b) Prevention of sore backs and girth galls.
      (i) Regular saddle may not fit properly when horse is first brought in. Saddle must not be too tight or pinch.
      (ii) When exercising, stay on level ground at first, or lunge horse to harden before riding.
      (iii) Treat back to speed up hardening process (lead lotion, salt and water or rubbing alcohol will harden skin).
      (iv) To prevent saddle rubbing, use a numnah.
      (v) If horse has sore place on back, use felt numnah with a hole cut out to fit over sore place.
      (vi) Harden skin on girth area in same way as back.
      (vii) Use mohair girth for first week or two.

   (c) Prevention of filled legs.
      (i) Filled legs caused by over-feeding. Do not increase grain too quickly.
      (ii) Feed damp hay and damp bran with three or four pounds of oats in two feeds or more, daily.
      (iii) Increase grain ration gradually according to exercise.

(iv) Feed bran and linseed mash frequently. Linseed must be properly cooked—otherwise poisonous. When cooked it forms a jelly and seeds sink to the bottom.

(v) If legs are filled, horse may need a physic.

(vi) Do not give physic unless absolutely necessary. If necessary, and horse is big and fat, he may need an "Aloes Ball" (5 grams). A lighter form of physic, also available in powder form, is a "Cupiss Ball". Stop grain, feed only hay and mash for twenty-four hours. When horse is over physic, start grain feeds again gradually.

WORMING

1. Horse should be wormed by veterinary surgeon, with stomach tube, when brought in.
2. If using a worming medicine administered in feed, use Equizole, or other brand recommended by veterinary surgeon.
3. Do not worm with Phenothiazine and then allow horse out in sunlight. He must be kept in for 48 hours, as there is a danger of dermatitis.

ACTUAL WORK AFTER BRINGING IN

1. First week—work on lunge with saddle and numnah. Protect back and girth area from sores.
2. Walking exercise, mounted, for second week, starting with quarter of an hour, increasing to three-quarters of an hour. If convenient, horse may be turned out for an hour or so daily in addition.
3. Third week—walk on hard ground, or road (harden tendons). Slow trotting up and down gentle slopes, gradually increasing distance in succeeding weeks.
4. Fourth and fifth weeks—continue work as in third week and introduce short canters. Gradually increase slow canters.
5. Two weeks later—breeze horse across fields two or three times during fortnight.

BIBLIOGRAPHY

First Aid Hints for the Horse Owner, W. E. Lyon.
The Manual of Horsemanship, B.H.S.

CHAPTER 18

THE TEETH AND AGEING

TYPES OF TEETH
1. Molars—grinding teeth.
2. Incisors—biting teeth.

The horse develops two sets of teeth: (a) temporary, milk, or deciduous teeth; and (b) permanent or persistent.

Molars

(a) There are twelve molars in each jaw—six each side.
(b) In temporary dentition only six molars—three each side.
(c) Molars form the sides of the dental arch—cheek teeth.

Incisors

(a) There are six incisors in each jaw.
(b) There are also six temporary incisors.
(c) The incisor teeth are situated in front.

Temporary teeth

Temporary, or milk teeth, are much smaller and whiter than permanent teeth.

Permanent teeth

Larger than temporary teeth and yellowish in colour.

Tushes or Canine teeth

(a) Two in each jaw of adult male. Do not usually occur in female.
(b) Tushes are situated a little further back in the jaw than the incisors. They occupy the space between the incisors and the molars.
(c) Tushes appear at $3\frac{1}{2}$ to 4 years and are fully developed at $4\frac{1}{2}$ to 5 years.

Wolf teeth

(a) Molar type teeth which frequently occur in the upper jaw, just in front of the molars.
(b) Wolf teeth have little root.
(c) They are a remnant of teeth well developed in the Eocene ancestor of the horse.
(d) Wolf teeth may erupt during first six months, and are often shed at the same time as the milk teeth behind them.
(e) If not shed, may remain indefinitely.
(f) Wolf teeth not shed should be removed by veterinary surgeon as the bit is inclined to catch on them.

1. *At birth*—two central incisors may be present, in each jaw. These may not appear until 7-10 days after birth. Three premolars—cheek teeth—are present in each side of each jaw.

2. *At two months*—the lateral incisors are present.

3. *At six months*—the corner incisors appear.

4. *At One Year*—all teeth are fully in wear, but corner incisors appear shelly (little wear on top). Four cheek teeth are present, the three premolars and the first permanent molar, which has just made its appearance through the gum.

5. *At Two Years*—Incisors showing signs of wear. The cup-like cavities on their tables have disappeared. Molars form a better guide. An additional permanent molar has made its appearance. There are now five cheek teeth present, three temporary premolars and two permanent.

   Confusion sometimes arises between a two-year-old and a five-year-old. In the case of the male, tushes or canine teeth will be present at five but not at two. The five-year-old will have six molars, the two-year-old, only five. The two-year-old will look young—tail may be shorter.

6. *At Two Years and Six Months*—permanent central incisors appear.

7. *At Three Years*—Permanent central incisors are in wear. First and second (in position counting from front) molars cut through gums, pushing out first and second temporary molars.

8. *At Three Years and Six Months*—Second pair of permanent incisors—the laterals—appear.

9. *At Four Years*—Permanent lateral incisors in wear.

10. *At Four Years and Six Months*—third pair of permanent incisors—the corner teeth—are cut. The last two permanent molars (numbers three and six in position counting from front) are cut between the ages of four and five years.

11. *At Five Years*—central and lateral incisors are in full wear. Corner teeth are well up and the inner and outer edges of their tables are level.

    Between four and five years, the tushes or canine teeth will appear in the male horse.

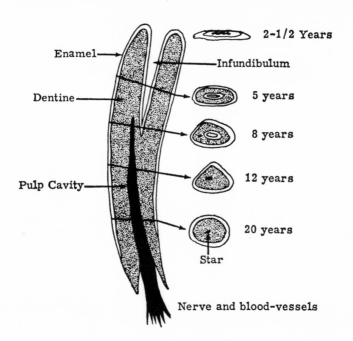

Enamel

Infundibulum

2-1/2 Years

Dentine

5 years

8 years

12 years

Pulp Cavity

20 years

Star

Nerve and blood-vessels

SIDEVIEW AND TOP OF TOOTH

12. *At Six Years*—Corner incisors now in wear. The infundibulum (the mark) of two central incisors may have entirely
disappeared. The 'dental star'—a brownish or blackish line
running transversely between the disappearing infundibulum and the anterior edge of the tooth—may sometimes
appear on the tables of the central incisors. This indicates
that the tooth has been worn away so as to bring the upper
extremity of pulp cavity, filled with dentine, into appearance.

13. *At Seven Years*—The infundibula have disappeared from
central and lateral incisors. Dental star may be present in
centrals. A hook appears at posterior edge of corner incisors
in upper jaw.

14. *At Eight Years*—The hook has gone. The infundibulum has
disappeared from all the incisors. Dental star clearly
apparent in central incisors.

15. *At Nine Years*—Dental star appears in lateral incisors. At ten
to twelve years it is present in all incisors.

117

16. *Shape of tables*—tables vary from oval, to triangular, to round, as horse gets older. Up to seven years tables are oval, from nine to thirteen years tables are triangular, after thirteen years tables are rounded and have a central pulp mark.

GALVAYNE'S GROOVE

A well marked, longitudinal groove, appearing on upper corner incisors. Appears as a notch just below the gum at nine or ten years and travels down the tooth. When groove reaches half way down tooth, horse is fifteen, when it has reached the bottom, horse is twenty. At twenty-five groove has disappeared from upper half of tooth, and at thirty it has disappeared completely.

Sidney Galvayne, horse expert and author of *The Twentieth-Century Book of the Horse,* first drew attention to this groove.

BISHOPING

The practice of tampering with the teeth to make an old horse appear younger. A false 'mark' is burned into the table of the tooth with a hot iron. Even the most expert bishoper cannot restore the enamel ring which surrounds the infundibular cavity, and which, in an old horse, will be absent.

LENGTH AND ANGLE OF TEETH

As the table of the tooth is worn out by friction, the alveolar cavity (fang hole), in which the root is embedded, is gradually filled up, so that the tooth is slowly pushed out from its socket. This continues throughout life and therefore, at successive periods, first the crown, next the neck, and finally the fang are actually in wear.

As the horse gets older, the teeth appear to be longer due to the recession of the gums. The setting of the teeth also becomes more oblique.

THE MARK OR INFUNDIBULUM

A dark depression on the tables of the teeth. It is surrounded by a distinct, narrow ring of enamel which is easily seen and felt. In the new tooth, the mark is broad and deep, but it disappears altogether with age and wear.

THE CROWN

The portion of the tooth which projects from the gum. It is covered at first with cement but this wears off to leave the enamel exposed.

THE FANG

The part of the tooth within the jaw. It is hollow and its cavity (the fang hole) contains blood vessels and nerves which make the tooth sensitive and also nourish it. The fang hole is gradually filled up with dentine of a lighter colour than the remainder and, when wear reaches this level, it appears on the table as a small white spot in the centre.

AGEING TERMS

Rising and Off—A horse is said to be "rising five" when he is nearer five than four. He is said to be "five off" when he is nearer five than six.

Aged—(a) In a sale catalogue means from eight years on up.

(b) In a racing catalogue means from six years on up.

Thoroughbreds are aged from January 1st each year.

Other horses are aged from May 1st each year.

TO 'FLOAT' TEETH

'Floating' teeth is rasping down the sharp edges which may appear periodically. The outer edges of the upper row of molars, and the inner edges of the lower molars, may become sharp with wear and cause injuries to the tongue and cheeks.

FULL MOUTH

This is the term employed to indicate that all the incisors are fully erupted—horse is five years old.

BLACK TEETH

A young horse with black teeth probably indicates that the feed is rich in iron.

WHITE TEETH

An older horse with white teeth indicates chalk in the feed.

GUMS

The gums recede with age. As they draw back they change the angle of the teeth. The top gum recedes before the bottom.

BIBLIOGRAPHY

Veterinary Notes for Horse Owners, M. Horace Hayes, pp. 512-526.

First Aid Hints for the Horse Owners, W. E. Lyon, pp. 119-124.

Manual of Horsemanship, The British Horse Society, pp. 252-253.

CHAPTER 19

THE FOOT AND SHOEING

STRUCTURE OF THE FOOT

The outside of the horse's foot, or hoof, is made of horn. The outer parts, though constantly growing, are virtually dead matter. This insensitive, horny covering of the sensitive structure of the foot may be divided into:

1. *The Wall*
This is the part seen when the foot is on the ground. It is composed of three kinds of horn:
    (a) Tubular horn—resembling fine fibres in appearance. Each tube grows from one tiny papillæ of the coronary band.
    (b) Intertubular horn—a glutinous horn substance also secreted by the coronary cushion. It cements horn tubes into solid-looking mass.
    (c) Intratubular or cellular horn—broken-down cells deposited inside the horn tubes. Function is to convey moisture.
    (i) The wall is approximately half an inch thick. It is thicker at the toes than the heels, but does not vary vertically.
    (ii) The wall grows constantly downward from the Coronet. For a new wall to grow from coronet to toe takes from nine to twelve months, and from coronet to heel takes from four to six months.
    (iii) The angle at which the front of the wall slopes should be 50° in the front feet and 55° in the hind feet.
    (iv) The outer layer of horn is known as the Periople. It is a thin, varnish-like horn which acts as a cover to protect the horn of the wall and prevent undue evaporation of moisture. The Periople is secreted from the papillæ of the perioplic ring which is situated round the upper border of the coronary band.

2. *The Sole*
Composed of similar horn to the wall, but is not constructed for sustaining weight, except at its junction with the Wall.

The Sole consists of two layers:

(i) Outer, or insensitive sole.

(ii) Inner, or sensitive sole—immediately above the insensitive sole and below the coffin bone. This sensitive sole is therefore between two hard substances and if subjected to undue pressure, it will be crushed and lead to great pain and lameness.

Undue pressure may be caused to the sensitive sole by:

(a) Paring of the outer, insensitive sole. Such paring renders the outer sole incapable of protecting the senstive sole.

(b) Mutilation of the crust (wall) and frog.

The sensitive sole feeds the horny sole, which grows from it and is constantly flaking away. Only these flaking pieces should be removed when preparing the foot for shoeing. The sole should not be pared away indiscriminately.

3. *The Frog*

The frog is composed more of the glutinous intertubular horn than of the tubular. It is tough and elastic. It does not support the Coffin Bone, which divides into the two processes which extend nearly to the heels. Between these processes is a large space, wherein lies the Plantar Cushion and below it the Frog. This gives the Frog great freedom of movement and provides the necessary elasticity of the back portion of the hoof. The Frog has five main uses, which can only be fulfilled if it is prominent and well developed:

(i) Shock absorber.

(ii) Anti-slip device.

(iii) Partial support for the Coffin Bone and especially a support to the Navicular Bone.

(iv) Heel expander. Every time the Frog comes to the ground, it bulges outwards, spreads the heels, and disperses the shock of impact outwards.

(v) Assists in circulation of the blood. Squeezes inner, sensitive parts of foot outwards against insensitive, unyielding horn, thus pumping blood back up veins of lower leg. Lack of pressure on the frog does not cut off blood supply to leg, but does impair it.

Obviously the Frog should not be pared, except in the case of disease. With natural use the Frog will become strong, and thrive. Without use it will shrink and eventually die.

4. *The Bars*

A continuation of the wall at the heel. They turn inward at the heel and continue alongside the frog to about half way to the point of frog, where they merge in the sole.

In preparing the foot for shoeing, the bars should not be pared away.

5. *The White Line*

A narrow ring or strip of horn between the sole and the wall, and forming the union of the two. It is soft, waxy horn of a lighter colour than the wall and sole.

6. *The Periople*

A thin, varnish-like horn which covers and protects the young horn of the wall.

7. *The Horny Laminæ*

Thin plates of horn standing at right angles to the interior surface of the wall. They interlock with the sensitive laminæ (fleshy leaves) which cover the pedal bone and lateral cartilages, to form a secure union of the sensitive foot to the hoof.

Approximately five to six hundred of each kind of laminæ are fitted into each hoof, thus giving a large bearing surface in a compact form.

8. *The Coronary Groove*

Runs around the top of the wall. The coronary cushion fits into this cavity. The cavity contains a large number of tiny holes, which are the start of the horn tubes of the wall. The papillæ of the coronary cushion fit into these holes, each one carrying on the work of secreting new horn. The wall grows downward from the coronary cushion. Injuries to the coronet may be followed by defects in the horn.

STRUCTURE OF THE FOOT—INTERNAL

1. *Bones*

The foot contains two-and-a-half bones:

(a) *The Coffin or Pedal Bone:*

Pyramid shaped, porous bone. Gives lightness to the foot, affords protection for the nerves and blood vessels it accommodates, its roughened surface affords ample attachment for the tendons, ligaments and sensitive laminæ.

(b) *The Navicular Bone:*

A small, triangular bone, like an elongated sesamoid, situated behind the joint of the Pedal Bone and the Short Pastern Bone. It acts as a rocker for the deep flexor Tendon. Its two rather pointed extremities are connected to the wings of the Pedal Bone by white, fibrous tissue.

(c) *The Short Pastern Bone:*

A nearly square bone to which the superficial flexor tendon and ligaments are attached. It articulates with the Pedal Bone and the Navicular Bone and is half inside and half outside the foot.

2. *Tendons*

There are three tendons in the foot, one in front and two at the back.

(a) *Extensor Tendon*

Originates from the muscles above the knee and hock. It runs down the front of the leg, over the fetlock and pastern joints, and is attached to the pointed centre of the upper border of the coffin bone. It straightens the limb and lifts the toe.

(b) *Superficial Flexor Tendon*

Runs down the posterior surface (back) of the cannon bone. Bends the leg and joints. It is attached to the lower part of the Short Pastern Bone.

(c) *Deep Flexor Tendon*

Runs down the back of the cannon bone, between the superficial flexor Tendon and the Suspensory Ligament. Bends the joint of the Coffin and Short Pastern Bones, passes under the Navicular Bone, and attaches to the lower part of the Coffin Bone. The deep flexor Tendon is broad and fan-shaped where it passes under the Navicular Bone and covers the Navicular completely, as if passing over a pulley.

3. *Ligaments*

Holds all bones securely in place and allow only the joints to move. The Suspensory Ligament occupies the space between the two splint bones and lies close behind the cannon bone. It divides into two strong bands, each of which attaches to the corresponding sesamoid bone. Some fibres pass on over the pastern and reinforce the Extensor Tendon.

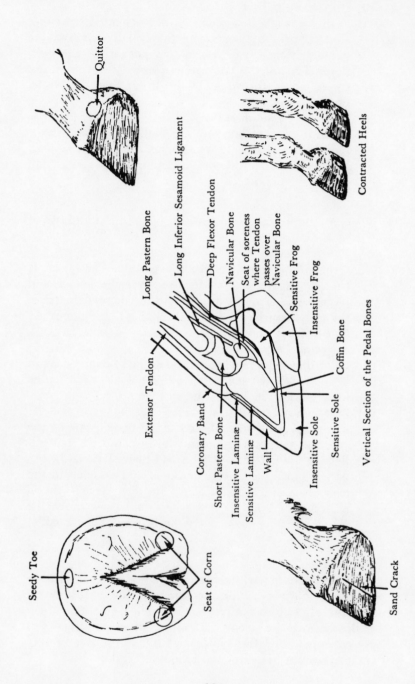

Quittor

Contracted Heels

Long Pastern Bone

Long Inferior Sesamoid Ligament

Deep Flexor Tendon

Navicular Bone

Seat of soreness where Tendon passes over Navicular Bone

Sensitive Frog

Insensitive Frog

Extensor Tendon

Coronary Band

Short Pastern Bone

Insensitive Laminæ

Sensitive Laminæ

Wall

Insensitive Sole

Sensitive Sole

Coffin Bone

Vertical Section of the Pedal Bones

Seedy Toe

Seat of Corn

Sand Crack

4. *The Lateral Cartilages*

Two flat pieces of gristle situated on each side of the foot and attached to the upper edge of the Coffin Bone. They act as protection to the Coronary Band and heel. The Lateral Cartilages stand up above the coronet about half an inch. They replace bones at the back of the foot, give elasticity to the hoof and reduce concussion. They are the flexible foundation of the wall and with the Frog and Plantar Cushion assist in expansion of the foot.

5. *The Plantar (Digital) Cushion*

A wedge-shaped mass of fibro-elastic tissue. It fills the space between the lateral cartilages and the wings of the coffin bone at the back of the foot. The plantar cushion extends forwards beneath the Navicular Bone. It is similar in shape to the Frog. It is a shock absorber, yielding upwards and outwards, forcing the heels apart and dispersing the jar of impact of the foot on the ground.

6. *The Coronary Cushion*

A fibrous band between the skin of the leg and the hoof. The flesh-like covering of the band, which is well supplied with blood, is attached to the upper part of the coffin bone and the extensor tendon. As it runs down the coffin bone, it becomes thinner, and ends in folds, which are the sensitive laminæ. The sensitive laminæ interlock with the horny laminæ of the hoof. There are between five and six hundred parallel pleats, plentifully supplied with blood. They form a secretory surface which helps to supply the substance to form the horn of the Wall.

7. *Nerves*

The foot is plentifully supplied with nerves.

8. *Blood supply to the Foot*

As a protection to the sensitive foot under pressure, there are no valves in the veins of the foot. The blood is entirely free and is pumped back up the leg by the pressure exerted when the sensitive foot expands on impact with the ground.

Blood is carried to the foot through arteries. The large metacarpal artery descends on the inner side of the leg. Just above the fetlock it divides into the digital arteries which then descend towards the wings of the coffin bone, where they divide again to supply the whole foot by means of an arterial circle known as the Plantar Circle.

The veins carry the used blood back to the heart, and so to the lungs to be purified. Blood and nerves give life and sensitivity to the foot. The volume of blood required by the foot to effect necessary repair is greater than that needed by the brain.

A horse of average size has approximately fifty pints of blood which circulates through its system every forty seconds.

SHOEING

1. Foot should receive attention every four to six weeks. If the foot gets too long, the toe turns up and the horse will stumble.

2. Hoof takes from nine to fifteen months to grow from top to bottom, therefore about one-ninth of the foot should be rasped off every month.

3. Test for lameness before taking horse to be shod and also after new shoes are fitted.

To Make the Shoe

1. Many blacksmiths now use ready-made, factory produced horse shoes. Disadvantages are:
   (a) Shoes come in set sizes and are not made to each individual foot.
   (b) Nail holes are all stamped in the same place. This means that nails are constantly driven through the hoof in the same spots, whereas a good blacksmith, making his own shoes, will vary the site of the nails.

2. If blacksmith makes his own shoes he buys the iron in bars, already concave and fullered (broader on the surface which is against the wall of the hoof, and grooved for added grip on the ground).

   (a) Suitable lengths of iron must be cut to make the new set of shoes.
   (b) The iron is made red hot in the fire and then shaped by use of the turning hammer on the anvil.
   (c) Nail holes are 'stamped' and toe clip 'drawn'.
   (d) Usual number of nails is four on the outside and three on the inside. The fewer nails used the better—on a healthy foot only two on each side may be necessary, but on an unhealthy foot up to six nails a side may be needed.

126

Actual Shoeing Operation

1. *Removal*

   Old shoe is removed. Using the buffer and shoeing hammer, the clenches are raised or cut off. Using the pincers and starting at the heel, the shoe is levered off the foot.

2. *Preparation*

   Consists of reducing the overgrowth of the wall to its natural length and trimming any ragged pieces from the sole and frog.

   (a) The hoof cutters are used in the case of excessive overgrowth of the wall.

   (b) Normally the "drawing knife" or "toeing knife" is used to trim the wall and remove ragged parts of the sole and frog. Undue use of the knife on sole or frog is harmful.

   (c) The rasp is then used to provide the foot with an absolutely level "bearing surface". The rasp is not used on the wall, except to make a nick under the nails before the clenches are turned down. A small piece is cut from the toe if the shoes are to have toe clips. Toe clips should not be hammered back when on the foot.

3. *Forging*

   This is the making of the new shoe and is described above. The weight and type of iron used will depend directly on the work required of the horse being shod.

4. *Fitting*

   In hot shoeing, fitting is done while the shoe is hot. It is carried, on a "pritchel", to the foot and held against the ground surface of the foot for a moment. The burning of horn which results shows the extent to which foot and shoe are in contact. Any adjustments necessary to the shoe—or the length of the heels—are then made.

   In the event that a fire and anvil are not available, the horse must be cold shod. The adjustments which can be made to a cold shoe are limited. Hot shoeing is preferable.

5. *Nailing*

   (a) The shoe is cooled by immersion in water.

   (b) The first nail driven is usually one of the toe nails.

   (c) Nails must be driven carefully and must be placed between the White Line and the outer edge. A nail too near the White Line will cause pressure, or nail bind. A nail driven inside the White Line causes a "prick".

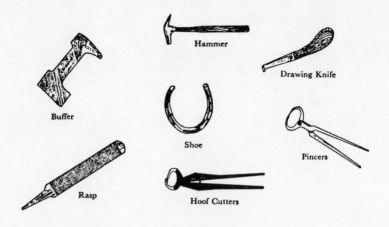

Hammer

Drawing Knife

Buffer

Shoe

Pincers

Rasp

Hoof Cutters

FARRIER'S TOOLS

(d) Nails should emerge one-and-a-half inches up the hoof.

(e) Specially designed nails are used and it is important to use the correct size nail.

(f) The end of the nail which penetrates the wall is twisted off, leaving a small piece projecting. This is called the "clench".

6. *Finishing*

(a) The clenches are smoothed with the rasp and a small "bed" made for them in the wall.

(b) The clenches are tapped down, tightened and given a final rasp to smooth them.

(c) The toe clip, or quarter clips, are lightly tapped back.

(d) The rasp is run round the lower edge of the wall to reduce the risk of any cracking in the wall.

What to look for in newly-shod foot

1. The shoe should have been made to fit the foot, not the foot to fit the shoe. That is, the wall should not have been rasped away to meet the iron and toe should not have been "dumped" (see Dumping, page 131).

2. The type of shoe provided should be suitable to the work required of the horse. The weight of iron should be in proper relation to the size of the foot.

3. The foot should have been suitably reduced in length at both toe and heel, and evenly on the inside and the outside.

4. The use of the knife on sole and frog should have been limited to light trimming only.
5. The frog should be in contact with the ground.
6. Sufficient nails should have been used (normally three on the inside and four on the outside). They should be the right size and the heads should be well driven home to fill the nail holes.
7. The clenches should be well formed, the right distance up the wall, and all in line.
8. No daylight should show between the shoe and the foot— pay particular attention to the heel region.
9. The heels of the shoe should be the correct length, neither too long nor too short.
10. The place for the clip should have been neatly cut and the clip well-drawn and well-fitted.

Indications that Re-shoeing is Necessary
1. There will be a sufficient growth of horn each month for the foot to require trimming even if the shoe is not worn.
2. The foot is overlong and out of shape.
3 The shoe is loose.
4. The shoe has worn thin—in any part.
5. The clenches are no longer close to the wall but have "risen".
6. A shoe has been "cast"—lost.

Types of Shoe
1. *The Plain Stamped Shoe*
   Simplest form of horse shoe. An unmodified bar of iron, shaped, stamped with nail holes and provided with toe clip. Only suitable for horse doing slow work. No provisions against slipping or interfering.
2. *The Hunter Shoe*
   Designed for a horse moving fast on grass and stopping suddenly and making sharp turns.
   (a) Made of "concave" iron—narrower below than above— to reduce the risk of suction in soft going and to provide a more secure grip on the ground.
   (b) Ground surface is "fullered"—provided with a groove— for better foothold.
   (c) Heels of the fore shoes are "pencilled"—smoothed off— to reduce the risk of the heel of the fore shoe being caught by the toe of the hind and torn off.

(d) The toe of the hind shoe is "rolled"—set back and bevelled off—to reduce risk of injury from over-reaching. Quarter clips are provided instead of toe clip, to allow for rolling.

(e) Outer heel of hind shoe is provided with a "calkin" to give better control in pulling up.

(f) Inner heel of hind shoe is provided with a "wedge" for the same purpose. A wedge is less likely to cause brushing than a calkin.

3. *The Feather Edged Shoe*

The inner branch of the shoe is "feathered"—reduced in width—and fitted close in under the wall. Reduces risk of injury from striking the opposite leg. There are no nail holes in the inner branch of the shoe.

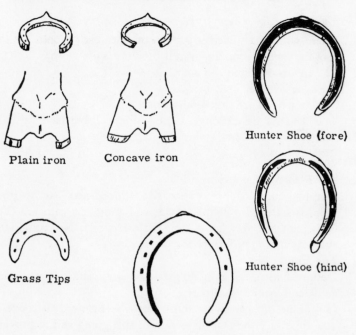

Plain iron

Concave iron

Hunter Shoe (fore)

Hunter Shoe (hind)

Grass Tips

Plain Stamped Shoe

4. *Grass Tips*

Thin, half-length shoes. Used on horses turned out to grass to protect the wall in the toe region from splitting. The frog is able to come into full action.

DUMPING

This is cutting back the toe of the foot to make it fit the shoe, instead of adjusting the shoe to fit the foot. This rasping of the surface of the wall removes the surface coat of the wall and exposes the horn. The horn becomes brittle and cracked and the rasped portions inevitably break away in time.

BLACKSMITH'S (FARRIER'S) TOOLS

1. *Driving hammer*
   For driving nails and twisting off their points when driven through the hoof.
2. *Buffer*
   Made of steel, it is about five-and-a-half inches long. Used for raising clenches.
3. *Rasp*
   About sixteen inches long and three-quarters coarse cut and one-quarter file cut.
4. *Drawing Knife*
   This knife has a curved blade with a bent over end. Used to trim wall and cut off ragged pieces of horn from sole and frog; also for cutting small pieces from the wall to provide seating for the toe clips.
5. *Pincers*
   Used to lever off the old shoe.
6. *Hoof Cutters*
   Shaped rather like pincers but with a flat end and overlapping blades, one thick the other thin. Used for trimming excessive overgrowth of the wall.
7. *Toeing Knife*
   Small steel knife with short, flat blade (like small axe-head). Also used, with hammer, to trim excessive overgrowth of wall.
8. *Pritchel*
   Steel instrument with pointed end which fits into nailhole in shoe. Pritchel can then be used as a handle to the hot shoe. Also used in fashioning the nail holes.

SURGICAL SHOEING

1. *Brushing*
   Usually occurs when toes turn out. Raise the inside of the shoe and use Feather Edged shoes. Or, lower the outside edge of the foot.

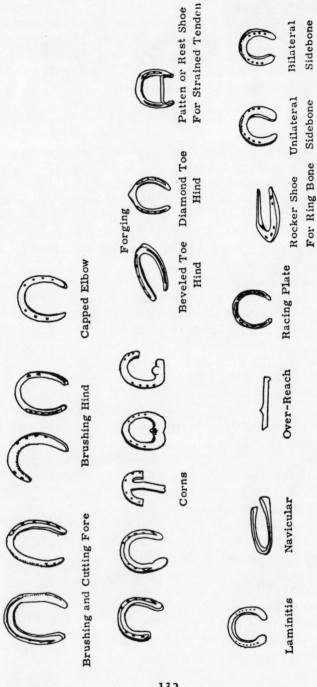

Brushing and Cutting Fore

Brushing Hind

Capped Elbow

Corns

Forging

Beveled Toe Hind

Diamond Toe Hind

Patten or Rest Shoe For Strained Tendon

Laminitis

Navicular

Over-Reach

Racing Plate

Rocker Shoe For Ring Bone

Unilateral Sidebone

Bilateral Sidebone

SURGICAL SHOES

132

2. *Capped Elbow*
   Shorten the heel. Use a three-quarter shoe with rounded edge. (To avoid necessity of three-quarter shoe, use stuffed sausage boot each night.)

3. *Contracted Heels*
   Shorten the shoe. Shoe with T-shoe. Additional pressure may be brought to the frog by use of a leather pad.

4. *Corns*
   Use bar shoe, designed to take the pressure off the affected part and on to the frog. A three-quarter bar shoe, a three-quarter shoe, and a shoe with set-down, thinned heels, all of which take the pressure off the affected part.

5. *Forging*
   Square the toe of the hind shoe and bevel it off. Set it back as far as possible. Diamond-toed hind shoes sometimes found effective.

6. *Injuries to the Back Tendon*
   Use a rest shoe built up at the back.

7. *Laminitis*
   Use a well seated out shoe, particularly seated out in toe area, to avoid pressure on the sole. (A seated out shoe is one in which the surface under the hoof is much narrower than the ground surface.) A shoe with a bar, which encourages frog pressure, may be helpful. According to the severity of the case, a leather sole may be helpful.

8. *Navicular Disease*
   Pressure must be removed from the deep flexor tendon at the point where it passes under the Navicular bone. Raise the heel with a graduated shoe which has a thin rolled toe, and thick heels. Recently, good results have been obtained with the use of a wedge-heeled pad placed under the shoe.

9. *Over-expanding Feet*
   Use heel nails.

10. *Over-reach*
    The toe of the hind shoe should be made square and wide and then rolled and set well back under the foot. The overhanging wall should be left on, just having the sharp edge blunted and left smooth with the rasp.

11. *Racing Plates*
    Light shoes for racing, made of aluminium and weighing between two and four ounces.

12. *Ringbone*

If disease affects front portion of the bones, as is more usual, wear will be on both heels. If the back part of the bones is involved, wear will be at the toe. For the former, shoe with a thin-heeled, bar shoe. For the latter, use an open rocker shoe (a shoe thin at the heel and the toe, on which the horse rocks). If frog pressure is required, use a rocker-bar shoe.

13. *Sidebone*

If the sidebone is on the outside edge, make the shoe much thinner and wider on the outside branch. The shoe should also be fitted wide on the outside and about five-eighths of an inch longer than the heel. In other cases, a rocker shoe, or a rocker-bar shoe is often successful.

14. *Speedy Cutting Wound*

A wound is inflicted either inside the knee, by the inside edge of the opposite fore foot; or inside the hock or thigh, by the outside edge of the front shoe on the same side.

In the first case, use a feather edged shoe, or a three-quarter shoe. In the second case, use a shoe with the outside edge feathered, or a three-quarter shoe with the space on the outside.

15. *Undercutting or Under-reach*

The toe of the hind foot is struck and injured by the toe of the fore foot as it is leaving the ground. Protection of the hind toe with a box clip may be necessary in extreme cases. This can often be avoided by fitting a fore shoe with a bevelled or sloped-off toe. The toe should be very open or square, with two clips, and should be set back, as with square-toed hind shoe. Bevelled-off portion at front causes the hind toe to be missed when in action.

BIBLIOGRAPHY

Veterinary Notes for Horse Owners, M. Horace Hayes, pp. 527-541 and 366-372.

First Aid Hints for the Horse Owner, W. E. Lyon, pp. 41-54, 76-77, 80 and 143-146.

The Manual of Horsemanship, British Horse Society, pp. 200-209.

Practical Farriery, C. Richardson.

The Foot and Shoeing, Major L. Davenport (a Pony Club Film Strip Book).

CHAPTER 20

DISEASES AND AILMENTS OF THE FOOT

PRICKS IN SHOEING

Causes:

1. Pricked Foot—nail is driven at the wrong angle and penetrates the sensitive part of foot.
2. Nail bind—nail is driven too close to the sensitive part of the foot but does not actually penetrate it. This may cause a bulge of the horn on to the sensitive structures which causes great pain.

Symptoms:

1. Lameness and localized tenderness over the site of the nail track.
2. A prick may not be noticed at once. Lameness may take days to appear.
3. Heat is usually present in the foot.
4. In all cases of obscure lameness the foot should be searched. This may be overlooked because of an enlarged fetlock which gives the impression of a sprain. Infection may be carried to the deep, sensitive parts of the foot along the track of a prick. If the prick is overlooked, it will become obvious after a few days by the appearance of an abscess on the coronet.

Treatment:

1. Each nail should be withdrawn and examined for moisture on the nail or oozing from the hole. The foot is a closed box and infection within the sensitive parts causes an inflammatory reaction, pain, and, usually, pus formation. As the pus increases the effects of pressure mount since it has no outlet.
2. When the offending nail has been found, the hole should be pared out to release the pus and allow constant, free drainage.
3. Apply hot, antiseptic poultices. Poultices (or hot fomentations in a tub) relieve pain and congestion and encourage the evacuation of pus.
4. After a few days poulticing the wound should be treated first with liquid antiseptic and later with Stockholm tar and tow.
5. If 'proud flesh' occurs as the wound heals it may be removed by the application of caustics. Daily application of lead and zinc paste (equal parts lead acetate and zinc sulphate ground together.

The grinding action causes the dry powders to become moist and they form a paste) for a few days will remove proud flesh without causing pain or damage to the horn.

6. In cases of 'nail bind' where lameness is slight and the sensitive foot has not been pierced, remove the shoe and poultice foot (or apply hot fomentations) for a few days to soften horn and reduce pressure effects. Later the nail hole should be filled with turpentine (which keeps it open and has a hardening effect). The horse must be rested until sound.

7. All cases of 'nail bind', pricks in shoeing or other forms of puncture wounds of the foot will necessitate complete rest for the horse until sound. Put horse on a laxative diet and substitute hay for grain.

WOUNDS OF THE SOLE AND FROG

Causes:
1. Punctures caused by stepping on nails, glass, etc.
2. Bruises from stones, hard ground, etc., are fairly common.

Symptoms:
1. Lameness—in the case of a picked up nail very sudden.
2. In the case of bruises to the sole, a flush of colour may be seen on the sole. The bruise is not in the horn of the sole but in the deeper, sensitive part of the foot covering the coffin bone.

Treatment:
Search foot. Treat as for nail pricks above.

CORNS

Causes:
1. Corns are bruises to that part of the sole in the angle of the wall and the bar.
2. May be caused by the structure of the foot—flat feet, weak heels, thin soles.
3. Or by poor shoeing—excessive paring of the sole, cutting away the bars, undue lowering of the heels. All such mistreatment of the foot tends to weaken the seat of corn and expose it to injury.
4. Front shoes too short—create pressure on seat of corn.
5. Shoes insecurely nailed, or loose shoes due to overgrowth of hoof, may be displaced and cause pressure and subsequently a bruise or corn.

Symptoms:
1. Ill-defined lameness—horse going short in front. (Corns rarely appear on hind feet.)

2. Severe pain and lameness; heat and tenderness.
3. Lameness increasing with work.
4. The existence of a corn is only known for certain when some of the horn is pared away from the sole around the seat of corn revealing a red spot, varying in size from a pea to a thumb nail.

Treatment:
1. The affected area must be pared as thin as possible. If the corn is an old one, discolouration will be near the surface; if it is new, it will be deeper, nearer to the sensitive parts of the foot.
2. If lameness is severe, or the corn is found to be suppurating, the foot should be poulticed, as described above under "pricks". When using a bran poultice, cover the corn with a pad to prevent bran from entering the wound.
3. In severe cases, as with "pricks", there may be swelling of the fetlock joint.
4. All pressure of the shoe must be removed from the seat of corn—use a three-quarter shoe.
5. Horse should be rested, and put on a laxative diet.
6. When foot is sound, particular care must be taken in shoeing to ensure that the shoe is the proper length. Leather or felt between the shoe and the sole, helps to minimize concussion.

QUITTOR
Causes:
1. Direct injury—i.e., a tread.
2. Indirect injury—i.e., following suppuration within the hoof caused by a corn, a prick, etc. The pus produced in such a case follows the line of least resistance and travels upwards to the coronet where it forms an abscess.

Symptoms:
1. Pain and lameness.
2. A tender area may be found on the coronet.
3. A tread may be suspected and appropriate treatment applied.
4. If the injury is deep-seated, there will be increasing lameness, heat, swelling and pain as the abscess forms.
5. When the abscess bursts there will be some relief. But the wound will not heal so long as the irritating portion of dead tissue remains within the foot.

Treatment:
1. If the injury is a simple tread, the pain should be relieved with poultices, footbaths, etc.

137

2. A raw area may occur due to local death of tissue at the site of injury. In this case, after poulticing, keep wound clean and protected until it heals.
3. If a quittor forms due to a deep-seated injury, treatment is more difficult. Poultice the wound. If damage to the sole can be found, pare away the sole and poultice.
4. Successful treatment depends on removing the dead tissue within the foot, which is often part of the lateral cartilage. This may require an operation and is definitely a case for the veterinary surgeon.
5. Horse will require complete rest and laxative diet.

THRUSH

A disease which affects the cleft of the frog.

Causes:
1. Excessive secretion from the glands deep in the cleft of frog.
2. Wet and dirt; neglected feet. Feet should be thoroughly picked out and washed or brushed clean at least once each day.
3. Standing on wet, dirty bedding.
4. Lack of use of the frog—incorrect shoeing, no pressure on the frog.

Symptoms:
1. There is a typical, offensive smell, caused by the bacteriological breakdown of the matter accumulating in the cleft of frog. (Excessive secretion from the skin glands.)
2. There is often a ragged appearance to the frog.
3. Slight cases of thrush rarely cause lameness, but severe cases may cause lameness.

Treatment:
1. The frog and its cleft must be thoroughly cleaned. Use a stiff brush and soap and water.
2. Loose and ragged pieces of the frog should be pared away.
3. In very bad cases it may be necessary to poultice the foot.
4. When the area is thoroughly clean and dry, dress with some simple astringent antiseptic: i.e., alum, calomel, sulphanilamide, or Stockholm tar.
5. Frog pressure is essential in all cases. Smear Stockholm tar on some tow and push it down into the cleft of the frog. This dressing can be kept in place by a leather sole or, if it must be changed often, by a piece of hoop-iron with its ends under the shoe.

6. Cases of thrush caused by lack of use of the frog must be treated similarly but in addition the foot must be gradually brought into use.

7. It may be necessary to remove the shoe and gradually lower the heels.

8. Shoeing with a shoe that is thin at the heels, or a bar shoe, may be necessary to bring the frog properly into use again.

9. In mild cases of thrush the horse should continue in work, since this will encourage more frog pressure.

10. If the ground is dry it is a good idea to turn the horse out. This achieves constant pressure on the frog and also provides the horse with 'green meat' which promotes the growth of healthy horn.

11. If the horse must be kept in, provide him with cod liver oil daily. This will also help promote the growth of healthy horn.

12. Many dressing are used successfully to cure thrush. No dressing will be effective without careful and constant attention to the cleanliness of the horse's feet and good hygiene in the stable.

CANKER

Canker is a chronic disease affecting the horn-secreting tissues of the foot. It is a foul-smelling, morbid condition, which starts at the sensitive frog and involves the sole, frog, and sometimes the wall.

Causes:

1. Not known, but it is often attributed to neglected thrush.

2. May arise from injuries to the foot, or from the downward extension of grease of the heel.

3. It may be attributable to some systemic or constitutional upset.

4. It may be attributable to invasion of the part by some germ or organism.

5. Bad hygiene favours the onset of the disease.

Symptoms:

1. First sign is usually a grayish-white, offensive discharge.

2. A soft, spongy swelling of the sensitive frog and sole develops and the horny covering breaks up.

3. The horn that is secreted is soft and cheese-like in texture.

4. The horn-producing power of the affected parts is ultimately destroyed. A thick flesh growth with a foul smell appears in its place.

5. Usually the condition is not painful and diseased horses may walk sound.

Treatment:
1. Canker must be treated at once to be successful. Those cases which have extended beyond the frog are very hard to cure.
2. Treat as for severe thrush.
3. Call the veterinary surgeon at once as an operation may be necessary.
4. Treatment is likely to be long and tedious.

SEEDY TOE

This condition arises when cavities form in the soft horn between the inner and outer parts of the wall. An unhealthy secretion of the sensitive laminæ prevents them from maintaining union with the insensitive layers. Cavities in the toe area are called 'seedy toe', in other areas of the foot they are called 'separation'.

Causes:
1. May be caused by injury to the coronet, which results in some aberration in the horn-secreting mechanism.
2. Pressure from the clip of the shoe, or blows to the wall, may be causes.
3. Irritation or inflammation of the sole, due to bruising, may interfere with the secretion of the white line and cause seedy toe.
4. Inflammation of the sensitive laminæ.
5. Diseased sensitive laminæ—as a result of laminitis.
6. Scalding with a hot shoe.
7. Bruising caused by working the horse unshod.

Symptoms:
1. Usually first seen by the blacksmith when removing the shoe.
2. A hollow cavity is found, filled with a soft, dark, cheesy type of material—broken-down horn.
3. If the hoof is tapped with a hammer it may give a hollow sound.
4. If the cavity extends deep into the foot it may become infected and pus may be produced.

Treatment:
1. The best treatment is to stimulate the growth of new horn and avoid all pressure at the point where the cavity makes contact with the shoe.

2. The cavity should be cleaned out thoroughly and packed with tow and Stockholm tar. Packing must be firm. It may be necessary to remove and renew it from time to time.

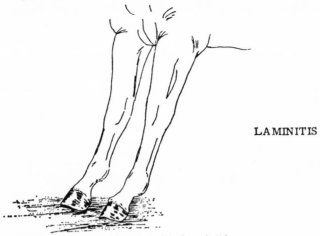

LAMINITIS

Typical stance of horse with Laminitis

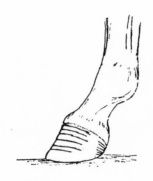

Hoof following Acute Laminitis

3. A mild blister may be applied to the coronet to stimulate growth of new horn.
4. Shoe with a light, bar shoe, thin at the heels to take the weight off the toe. Or shoe with a seedy toe shoe which prevents the injured part from bearing any weight.
5. Turn the horse into lush pasture—the spring grass will often work wonders on the promotion of new horn growth.

LAMINITIS (also called Founder or Fever of the Feet)

Painful state of congestion affecting the vascular system within the hoof. The congested tissues provide ideal conditions for invading organisms and inflammation of the sensitive laminæ often follows. The original attack is always acute and may be entirely relieved with no permanent ill effects. If the disease progresses to the point where changes in the structure of the foot occur, the result is known as chronic laminitis.

Causes:
1. Excessive work—especially if horse is unfit.
2. Concussion—long, fast driving, or riding (particularly if the sole and frog have been cut away impairing the shock absorbancy of the foot).
3. Heredity or malconformation—wide, flat feet and weak horn.
4. Idleness and lack of exercise—horses kept stabled without proper exercise (as on a long sea voyage) especially if fed on a diet well beyond maintenance requirements.
5. Digestive disturbance — high feeding, too much grain (especially heating grain, barley, wheat, beans, etc.).
6. Debilitating diseases — e.g., influenza, which weakens the action of the heart.
7. Difficult foaling—which may cause general disturbance of the vascular system.
8. Undue weight placed on one or more feet—e.g., horses in pain as a result of accident to one limb may place unusual weight on the other front leg. If continued for a long time this may give rise to a state of congestion and ultimately laminitis in the weight-bearing limb. Always support both front legs with bandages if one is injured.
9. Too much spring grass—grass laminitis often affects small ponies who will eat without ceasing as long as they are able. Keep ponies in during the day and only turn out to grass at night.

Symptoms
1. Attack is sudden. Acute pain and lameness, horse can hardly be made to move.
2. Heat in front part of feet. Tapping the affected foot, or feet, with a light hammer gives rise to pain.
3. Horse adopts typical posture, feet stretched forward, weight on the heels in an attempt to relieve the pressure. (Almost always it is the front feet which are affected.)

4. Difficult to pick up feet—horse is unwilling to put weight on other affected feet.
5. Laminitic ridges on the hoof—rougher and less regular than grass rings—may form due to the horn being produced at an inconstant level.
6. Horse may lie down flat on his side to relieve pressure. If left lying down he must be turned frequently from side to side to avoid dangers of other diseases due to passive congestion.

Treatment

1. Laxative diet.
2. Initially the congestion, pressure and pain must be relieved. Methods include bleeding at the toe, injection of adrenaline (in vicinity of arteries above the foot to reduce local arterial blood supply), etc. Veterinary advice is essential.
3. Ice cold poultices applied to the feet, or standing the horse in ice cold water may relieve congestion.
4. Alternate hot and cold poultices are often effective.
5. As soon as acute pain has subsided, the horse should be exercised. Shoe with a bar shoe, or special laminitis shoe, which keeps pressure from the sole. All weight is borne on the wall and frog, and heels.
6. In favourable cases, quickly treated, the foot may not suffer too much deformity. Otherwise due to pressure within the foot, the pedal bone is turned on its horizontal axis. The toe is said to "drop" causing the sole to lose its dome and become flat, or even bulge downwards.
7. Once the sole has dropped the condition is known as 'chronic laminitis' and the horse may only be made usable again after months of careful trimming and shoeing. He will then only be useful for quiet work.
8. In cases where inflammation has not been too severe (and in grass laminitis promptly treated) the horse will become sound again.

GRASS RINGS

Ridges sometimes appear in the wall, particularly when horses are at grass. This condition is caused by differences in growth rate of the horn. This is not serious, and not to be confused with laminitic ridges, which are rougher and more irregular and tend to merge together towards the heel.

NAVICULAR DISEASE

A disease process involving the navicular bone. Changes occur in the bone including an increase in size, discolouration and ulceration of the posterior surface. The deep flexor tendon glides over the posterior surface of the navicular bone. The roughened bone surface causes pain and lameness.

Causes:

1. Concussion has been the accepted cause for many years, but since the navicular bone is well protected against concussion, this may not be the true cause.
2. Compression of the navicular bone by the deep flexor tendon (causing disturbance of the blood supply to the bone) is another possible cause.
3. Direct injury.
4. Hereditary predisposition.
5. Bad shoeing, high heels, etc.
6. Rheumatism.
   Have all been suspected causes.

Symptoms:

1. Sudden, probably quite severe, lameness.
2. Lameness disappears, or becomes very slight.
3. Horse may be restless and uneasy on his feet in the stable. Later he will point. If both fore feet are affected, he will point first one and then the other.
4. Horse travels best up hill. May be lame coming out of the stable but warm out of it with exercise. However, if put away and left to cool, and then taken out of the stable again, lameness may be more pronounced for the first few steps.
5. As the disease develops the hoof alters shape. This is nature's attempt to relieve the pressure on the affected part. Hoof becomes "blocky" (deep at the heel and short at the toe, raising the sole and frog from the ground).

Treatment:

1. If recognized early and steps are taken to relieve pressure and tension, there is a chance of cure.
2. The toe should be shortened and the heel allowed to grow deep. Sole should be pared to produce springing action, to compensate for the loss of the pumping action of the frog.
3. Shoe with a graduated shoe, with thin rolled toe and thick heels. This lessens the angle of the tendon and reduces pressure where the tendon passes under the navicular bone.

4. Branches of the shoe should be as narrow as possible so that the wall bears all the weight.
5. Horse should be kept up, well fed, and given 'green meat' and one-third of a pint of cod liver oil daily. This will help promote a good growth of horn.
6. Exercise should be at the walk, under saddle. The action is thus controlled and exercise ensures good circulation within the foot.
7. In long-standing cases, where the hoof has already become 'boxy', hoof section may be performed and give immediate relief.
8. Cortisone injections may be used to relieve pain and lameness and may work for a while.
9. Neurectomy (denerving)—severing of certain selected sensory nerves within the foot—will relieve pain and lameness when all other means fail.
10. Neurectomy does not, in most cases, deprive the foot of all sensation. It is looked on as 'dangerous' and 'dishonest' by many horsemen, but it is widely practiced in certain areas and many de-nerved horses have been hunted, show jumped and steeplechased for years, free from pain and lameness.
11. If a de-nerved horse comes up for sale it must be disclosed that the operation has been performed. He is legally unsound.

PEDAL OSTITIS

Bruising of the pedal bone. Very common in riding horses and race horses.

Causes:
1. Continued concussion.
2. The laminæ and sensitive sole may be involved and there may be a mild degree of laminitis.

Symptoms:
1. Lameness—varies in degree but is usually not severe, though sufficient to keep the horse from work.
2. Common in the fore feet and rare in the hind feet.
3. Horse is tender on his feet, and goes short.
4. Pain will be accentuated by trotting him on loose gravel and he may go very lame.
5. Heat in the foot. Flinching from hoof testers, or light taps with hammer.
6. May be evidence of bruising of the sole.

7. Lameness may work off with light exercise but will return more acutely if horse is rested and then brought out cold.
8. X-ray will confirm the diagnosis.

Treatment:
1. Turn out on soft land for six months or more.
2. Frequent attention to the feet is essential. Keep shod with light, wide-webbed shoe. No pressure on the sole. Heels should be deepened and toe dumped to produce slight rocker effect.
3. Give plenty of walking exercise under saddle.
4. Good feeding, including cod liver oil and green food essential.
5. Soft ground is vital, hard ground will accentuate the trouble.

SANDCRACK

Symptoms:
1. A vertical splitting of the wall of the hoof.
2. Vary in length and depth, true sandcrack extends from the upper to the lower border of the wall.
3. Usually occur on the inside quarter of the fore foot and in the toe of the hind.
4. Begins as a small fissure close to coronet and extends upwards, downwards and inwards.
5. Does not usually cause lameness, unless deep enough to expose the sensitive laminæ.

Causes:
1. Weak, brittle feet.
2. Concussion (in the fore), or strain (in the hind) from heavy loads.
3. Injury (i.e., a tread) to the coronary band.
4. Rasping the wall.

Treatment:
1. If Sandcrack is deep and exposes the sensitive tissues, these become liable to injury. The injury may be simple pinching or more serious infection and inflammation. In this case there will be considerable pain and lameness.
2. Pain and inflammation must be treated first. Poultice foot for two or three days. This removes foreign matter and pus.
3. Prevent movement. Crack may be immobilized by riveting the edges firmly together with a horse shoe nail driven horizontally and clenched at each end.

4. Shoe with a flat shoe. If crack is at the toe do not use a toe clip, but draw two small clips, one on each side of the toe. This will help to prevent movement of the divided wall.

5. Remove a portion of the wall at the bottom of the crack before shoeing. This will ensure that no pressure exists between the affected part of the wall and the shoe. Such pressure would tend to force the crack open wider.

6. The growth of new, sound horn must be encouraged. The repeated application of a mild blister to the coronet combined with good feeding, adding cod liver oil to the feed, and feeding new spring grass, will all help.

7. Granulation tissue (proud flesh) may form and protrude from the crack, if the deep sensitive tissues were the site of infection. Daily application of a caustic or astringent dressing (silver nitrate, copper sulphate, etc.) will remove this tissue apparently painlessly.

8. If the crack is discovered in the early stages and is not deep, some control can be effected by burning grooves into the wall with a hot iron. Grooves may be made transversely across the crack, or across the wall above and below the crack, and also in the shape of a V. The apex of the V may coincide with the lower limit of the crack and the sides slope up towards the coronet, or the V may be inverted so that the sides slope towards the lower border of the hoof. The grooves should be as deep as possible without damaging inner sensitive structures. The object is to divert concussion from the weak area to a strong area of the wall.

SPLIT HOOF

Splits or fissures in the wall, beginning at the lower border and extending upwards, are generally the result of direct injury. They are usually superficial and shallow. Often seen in horses turned out without shoes, and when feet are neglected. Treat as for sandcrack which has not reached the coronet. Prevent splits by trimming feet regularly and providing correct diet.

BIBLIOGRAPHY
Veterinary Notes for Horse Owners, M. Horace Hayes, pp. 187-219.

Practical Farriery—a Guide for Apprentices and Junior Craftsmen, C. Richardson, Pitman, pp. 34-46.

First Aid Hints for the Horse Owner, W. E. Lyon, pp. 41-52.

CHAPTER 21

INTERFERING

BRUSHING

At any pace faster than a walk, the horse's opposite limbs hit one another alternately, usually at the fetlock, occasionally at the coronet.

Causes:

1. Bad conformation.
2. Bad action.
3. Horse is young and green, or old and weak.
4. Horse is overtired, or overworked, or underfed.
5. Prominent clench.
6. Ill-fitting shoes, or shoes which are too heavy.

Treatment:

1. Discover the cause and if possible remove it.
2. If cause is youth and greenness of horse, use brushing boots or Yorkshire boots during schooling for a few weeks until horse gains more muscle tone.
3. Adjust shoeing—shoe with feather edged shoe (inner branch very strong and built up, with no nail holes), or, in the case of a hunter, with a flat shoe fitted close under the wall on the inside, or a three-quarter shoe.

SPEEDY CUTTING

Term applied to injury inflicted by the opposite limb just below the knee. The blows are more severe and inflict a wound. Rare, except in high-stepping trotters or horses being forced over heavy going when unfit or unbalanced. Treat as for Brushing.

OVER-REACHING

An injury to the back of the fore leg (usually in the heel area) caused by the toe of the hind shoe. Damage is caused by the inner margin of the toe of the hind shoe and not by the front of the toe.

Causes:

1. Fore limb insufficiently extended, or hind limb over-extended.
2. Galloping and jumping in heavy going.
3. Careless riding.

Treatment

1. Apply iodine at once. On returning to the stable, treat as bruised wound. Wounds vary in severity from slight bruising to deep cuts.
2. The toe of the hind shoe must be made wide and square and well concaved on its inner surface. Shoe must be placed well back at the toe with the clips let into the wall and flush with it. The wall at the toe should be left on but blunted with the rasp.
3. Horses liable to over-reach should wear over-reach boots when hunting or jumping.

FORGING

Occurs at trot when the toe of the hind shoe strikes the underneath surface of the corresponding front shoe.

Causes:

1. Young, green horse which promises to be a 'goer'.
2. Bad riding (insufficient attention to rhythm).
3. Bad conformation—over sloping pasterns.
4. Feet too long in the toe.

Treatment:

1. If due to youth, forging will disappear when horse is older and in better condition and can be ridden up to his bit.
2. Shoe fore feet with concave shoes to assist horse in getting front feet out of the way quickly.
3. Hind shoes should be made with square toes and set well back under the wall at the toe.
4. Flat hind shoes with heels slightly thinner than the toes will help by retarding the forward movement of the hind foot.

UNDERCUTTING

Injury to the toe of the hind foot, caused by the toe of the front foot scraping it as the front foot comes up from the ground.

149

Causes:

1. Peculiarity of the action—perhaps caused by very compact, short-backed conformation.

Treatment:

1. Shoe the front feet with square toed, bevelled off shoe with two clips. Set shoe well back under the wall at the toe. This causes front toe to miss toe of hind foot when horse is in action.
2. In serious cases, protect hind toe with a box clip. This added weight also retards the forward movement of the hind foot and helps to avoid contact with the fore foot.

BIBLIOGRAPHY

Veterinary Notes for Horse Owners, M. Horace Hayes, pp. 366-372.

Practical Farriery—a Guide for Apprentices and Junior Craftsmen, C. Richardson, Pitman, pp. 47-53.

First Aid Hints for the Horse Owner, W. E. Lyon, pp. 76-77 and 80.

Horsemen's Veterinary Adviser, Joseph B. Davidson, pp. 73-74.

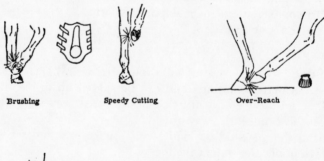

Brushing   Speedy Cutting   Over-Reach

Undercutting

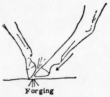

Forging

CHAPTER 22

DISEASES OF THE BONE

SPLINTS

Bony enlargement on the cannon bone or the splint bones or between any of the three bones. Usually on the inside of the fore-leg, but sometimes on the outside. More often on the fore-limbs but occasionally on the hind.

Causes:
1. Periostitis—inflammation of the bone skin—caused by:
   (a) Concussion—perhaps provoked by bad conformation.
   (b) Strenuous work too early, with too much weight inflicted on immature limbs.
   (c) Blows inflicted by one foot on the opposite leg.

Symptoms:
1. Horse usually walks sound but trots lame.
2. Lameness increases with work.
3. Usually obvious to sight and touch—but not always.
4. Pressure of the fingers on the seat of disease causes pain.

Treatment:
1. Once formed, splints generally cause little trouble.
2. Formation rare in horses over six years old.
3. Much depends on the site of the splint. If formed on the cannon bone, or splint bones, out of the way of the knee and fetlock joints and the tendons, they cause little trouble. High splints may affect the action of the knee. Splints positioned far back may interfere with the free movement of the tendons.
4. While splint is forming rest horse and put on laxative diet.
5. Hose with cold water for fifteen minutes three times a day (or stand in cold stream).
6. Apply cold water bandages or cooling lotion between periods of irrigation.
7. Ensure that horse is shod so that there is pressure on the frog. Leather between the shoe and the wall will help to reduce concussion.

8. If lameness persists after two weeks, apply a blister.
9. A splint can be pin-fired, if lameness is persistent, with great success.
10. Exercise should be very light. If sound at walk, give walking exercise. If horse is worked during formation of splint, a very large splint will be the result.
11. Splint formation is very common in horses under six years. Young horses have more lime in bloodstream as bones are still forming. Tendons and ligaments are less able to absorb shock and concussion than in an older horse. Bad bruising slows circulation causing lime deposit to form.
12. Average cases go sound in four to six weeks and have no further trouble with the splint, unless it is so large that it causes interference. In this case it can be removed surgically.
13. Many splints are absorbed in later life and disappear.

BONE SPAVIN

Bony enlargement on the lower, inner aspect of the hock.

Causes:
1. Heredity—sickle hocks and cow hocks are susceptible.
2. Immaturity—working horse too hard too young.
3. Severe exertion—jumping out of heavy going, pulling up suddenly, drawing heavy loads.
4. Any undue concussion, particularly if horse is unfit or over-tired.

Symptoms:
1. Lameness, either slight or severe. Increases initially after short rest, but diminishes with exercise.
2. Horse takes short stride with affected leg. Marked stiffness in affected joint which causes dragging of the toe.
3. The quarter of the affected leg drops when the foot comes to the ground.
4. Turning in a small circle with affected leg on the outside increases the lameness and horse has a jerky way of taking the foot off the ground.
5. Lameness may disappear after a few months but if the horse stands for a while, after exercise, and then is moved again, increased stiffness will be apparent.

152

Treatment:

1. Rest and laxative diet.
2. Apply hot fomentations until inflammation has subsided.
3. Follow up with cold water irrigation for a few days.
4. Blistering the seat of spavin, and repeating the treatment every three weeks for five or six times, is sometimes effective.
5. Pin firing gives the most consistent good results.
6. One month after firing, re-apply red blister.
7. Blistering and firing should be followed by a long rest out at grass.
8. Shoe with high heel (wedge heel, not calkins) and roll the toe. This rests affected joint.

OCCULT SPAVIN

Name given to bone spavin which occurs between the articular surfaces of the bones of the hock joint. No bony enlargement is visible. Causes as for Bone Spavin.

Symptoms:

1. As for Bone Spavin, but no bony enlargement visible.
2. Lameness does not diminish with exercise. Degree of lameness may vary, but horse is constantly lame and lameness may become more pronounced with exercise.
3. More heat noticeable in affected hock.

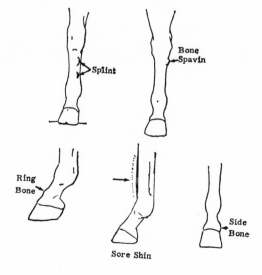

Treatment:

1. Likely to be very long (at least eight months) and the horse may be permanently crippled.
2. Line fire right round the joint and also apply blister.
3. Repeat blister every four weeks for three or four months.
4. Keep horse at rest in loose box during treatment. After four months, turn out to grass for several months more, if possible.
5. Shoe with high-heeled shoe to rest joint.
6. Treatment must be regarded as speculative.

RINGBONE

Bony enlargement resulting from an ostitis of the upper or lower pastern bones. Two classifications—high ringbone, involving the long pastern bone—or low ringbone, involving the short pastern bone. Either classification may, or may not, involve the joint.

Causes:

1. Poor conformation—upright or over-long pasterns.
2. Concussion, sprains and blows.
3. Shoes left on too long, allowing heels to grow too long. This removes frog pressure and increases jar on the feet.

Symptoms:

1. If ringbone involves a joint, the horse may come out slightly lame, and lameness will persist.
2. Heat and pain will not be present for a week or two.
3. As with other bony enlargements, horse will be more lame on hard ground than on soft.
4. Fetlock joint will lack flexion.
5. If ringbone does not involve a joint, there will be no lameness.
6. In later stages the enlargement may be felt—in the case of high ringbone, around and above the coronet.
7. Low ringbone in the later stages changes the shape of the hoof. The exostosis appears in front of the coffin bone, and in long-standing cases the wall will show a ridge.

Treatment:

1. Rest and laxative diet.
2. Reduce inflammation with cold water irrigation.
3. Shoe with thin heeled, bar shoe, if horse is going on his heels.
4. If disease is at the toe, fit an open rocker shoe. If joint is stiff, use rocker or rocker bar shoe.
5. Blistering or pin firing may prove effective.
6. Cortisone injections are the latest treatment and may be effective.
7. If the ring bone involves a joint the horse will probably be incurably lame.

SORE SHINS

Inflammation of the periostium (membrane covering the bone) in the front of the cannon bone. Common in young race horses.

Causes:

1. Concussion—galloping on hard ground.

Symptoms:

1. Horse goes short, usually in both fore limbs, and may or may not be lame.
2. Heat and tenderness on the front of the cannon bone.
3. Painful, diffuse swelling occurs on the front of the cannon bone.
4. Legs may become enlarged.
5. Loss of freedom of action in both fore limbs. If work continues, lameness will result.

Treatment:

1. Rest and laxative diet.
2. Apply hot packs or poultices (antiphlogistine or animalintex) to relieve pain.
3. After two or three days change to cold water irrigation.
4. Continue to apply cold water bandages for a week or two, even after starting work. Helps tone up the legs.
5. In bad cases, where there is a bony deposit, the legs should be blistered.

SIDE BONES

Ossification of the lateral cartilages of the foot.

Causes:
1. May be hereditary.
2. Result of inflammation of the lateral cartilages caused by concussion.
3. May result from a blow or a tread.
4. Undue concussion fostered by thick-heeled shoes or calkins.

Symptoms:
1. Can be felt. In 'partial' side bone, a portion of the cartilage remains flexible, whilst the other portion is resistant. In 'complete' side bone there is no flexibility.
2. Lameness is not generally present unless some other condition (e.g., ring bone) is also affecting the limb.
3. The side bones may not cause lameness, but a contracted foot, causing pressure on the sensitive parts by squeezing them between the pedal bone and the ossified cartilage and the wall of the hoof, will cause pain and lameness.
4. In cases of unilateral side bone (which usually occurs on the outside) the shoes will wear more on the outside branch.

Treatment:
1. If no lameness is present, none is indicated.
2. If horse is lame, rest and cold applications are indicated.
3. Special shoeing may relieve pressure, and expand hoof.
4. Blistering, and/or firing may be helpful.
5. If lameness persists, the veterinary surgeon may perform an operation known as grooving the wall. This relieves the pressure which is causing the lameness.

BIBLIOGRAPHY

Veterinary Notes for Horse Owners, M. Horace Hayes, pp. 450-452, 472-475, 458-460, 456-457 and 463-464.

Practical Farriery, C. Richardson, pp. 28-34, 45-46.

First Aid Hints for the Horse Owner, W. E. Lyon, pp. 52-55, 58-60, 63-64.

Manual of Horsemanship, B.H.S., pp. 232-238.

Horseman's Veterinary Adviser, J. B. Davidson, pp. 94-101, 189-192, 196-197.

CHAPTER 23

SPRAINS

SPRAINS

A sprain is an injury to a ligament, tendon, muscle or a joint which involves laceration of the fibres and sometimes stretching. There may also be a displacement of parts (sprains to joints).

"Sprained Tendons" is a loosely applied term and generally refers to a rupture of some of the ligamentous attachments of the tendon sheath. Tendons are made of totally inelastic tough white cords. On the rare occasions when the tendon itself is strained or stretched it remains stretched, because, being inelastic it cannot retract. This condition is known as a bowed tendon.

Causes:
1. Pulling a horse up suddenly, as in polo.
2. All the weight of the body coming on one leg.
3. Too much galloping (e.g., a race horse in training).
4. Galloping or jumping in heavy going, especially when the horse is tired.
5. Allowing the toes to get too long.
6. Defective conformation—e.g., long, sloping pasterns; a crooked leg; tied in below the knee.
7. Ringbone, or enlarged pasterns, which restrict the free movement of the joints. This may mechanically cause the relaxation of the tendons.
8. Rarely sprains may be caused by horse slipping or getting cast in stable.

Symptoms—General:
1. Lameness—suddenly manifested.
2. Pain, heat and swelling—diffuse at first, becoming better defined later, around the tendons.

Symptoms of injury to the Flexor Tendons:
1. Lack of flexion of the knee when in motion.
2. Inability to raise and flex the leg, resulting in dragging of the toe.
3. When standing, horse keeps knee slightly bent and heel off the ground, to relax the tendon.
4. Injury to deep flexor tendon, or check ligament, involves a great deal of pain.

5. When deep flexor tendon is involved, swelling is at the side of the leg.

6. When injury is to the superficial flexor tendon, swelling, or curve, is at the back of the leg.

7. When check ligament is injured, there is little external swelling or heat. However, horse will flinch as he puts the foot to the ground, due to the weight coming suddenly on to the injured ligament.

8. When suspensory ligament is injured there is seldom much swelling.

Diagnosis of Seat of Sprain:

1. Lift the foreleg and press the various tendons with finger and thumb until the horse flinches.

2. To test check ligament, apply pressure by lifting the foot and bending it right back (under elbow). In this position the ligament can be felt.

Sprained Tendon

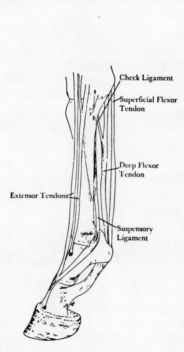

Check Ligament

Superficial Flexor Tendon

Deep Flexor Tendon

Extensor Tendons

Suspensory Ligament

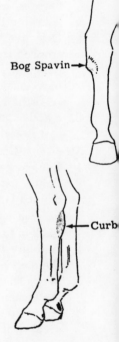

Bog Spavin →

← Curb

3. Test suspensory ligament in the same way as check ligament.
4. If the swelling over the tendons 'pits' on pressure from the tips of the fingers, the swelling is *not* due to sprain.
5. Lameness, heat, and swelling of the limb in the region of the tendons, may be due to causes other than sprains, e.g., infection and pus in the foot, compression from a rope round the limb, a blow from the opposite foot.
6. If in doubt, remove the shoe and exclude the possibility of the cause of lameness being in the foot before treating as for sprain.

Treatment—General, for all Sprains:

1. Complete rest and laxative diet (no grain).
2. If injury is slight, cold water bandages, or support bandages over lead lotion (cooling) may be all that is necessary.
3. Usually injury is more severe. Inflammation and tenderness must be removed by poulticing (Antiphlogistine or Animal-intex).
4. After three days of hot poulticing, hose frequently with cold water and apply cotton wool soaked in lead lotion and bandage for support.
5. Fit a patten shoe—made by raising the heels and fitting a wide bar across the top of them. The bar ensures comfortable bearing on any floor. High heel rests tendon. Gradually reduce height of heel as recovery progresses.
6. In severe cases, blistering or firing may be necessary, followed by a long rest.

After Treatment for Sprains:

1. After a serious sprain, a horse requires a minimum of six months rest before going back to hard work.
2. Hand rubbing of the tendons is beneficial.
3. Embrocation (an ointment or liniment) may be beneficial as a stimulant combined with hand rubbing.
4. Lower heels of shoe gradually. After the patten shoe, wedge heels may be used and the height gradually reduced. (Calkins are not good as they sink into small holes in floor and do not give even support.)
6. Bring horse back into work gradually.

CURB

An enlargement, approximately five inches below the point of hock. Either a thickening of the sheath of the deep flexor tendon, or an enlargement of the ligament uniting the bones of the hock.

Causes:

1. As for sprains.
2. Jumping badly, or out of deep going.
3. Weak hocks, or sickle hocks are liable to curb.

Symptoms:

1. A curved, convex enlargement is visible when hock is viewed from the side. May be very slight and found only on manipulation.
2. Heat and pain are usually present.
3. Horse may or may not be lame. If lame he will go on his toe and when standing will raise heel off the ground.

Treatment:

1. Rest and laxative diet.
2. Shoe with wedge-heeled shoe.
3. Treat as for sprains.
4. An embrocation or mild blister may be applied.
5. In bad cases, where conformation of hocks makes them prone to curb, firing will usually be a permanent cure.

BIBLIOGRAPHY

Veterinary Notes for Horse Owners, M. Horace Hayes, pp. 452-456 and 478-479.

Practical Farriery—a Guide for Apprentices and Junior Craftsmen, C. Richardson, Pitman, pp. 18-21.

First Aid Hints for the Horse Owner, W. E. Lyon, pp. 56-58 and 61-62.

Horsemen's Veterinary Adviser, Joseph B. Davidson, pp. 69, 103 and 107.

The Manual of Horsemanship, The British Horse Society, pp. 236-237.

CHAPTER 24

BURSAL AND SYNOVIAL ENLARGEMENTS

DEFINITION

Enlargements or distentions of the synovial membrane which encloses all true joints, and certain parts of all tendons and some ligaments. An increased secretion of synovia, or joint oil, Nature's provision to lessen irritation, causes the enlargements.

When over`exertion or strain produce irritation, the synovial membrane is excited to increase secretion of oil.

Horses with upright shoulders, fetlocks or hocks (i.e., with conformation lacking in elasticity of the joints) are most liable to synovial enlargements. Classified under this general heading are Thorough-pin, bog spavin, wind-galls, etc.

TREATMENT—GENERAL NOTES

1. Treatment must depend on cause. Those enlargements caused by work and concussion may be cured but are likely to reappear.
2. Enlargements caused by accidents, sprains or ligaments or parts of the tendons, are not so likely to reappear once they have been reduced.
3. Rest and laxative diet.
4. Friction and pressure help by stimulating the action of the blood vessels.
5. Horses showing much wear benefit from hosing with cold water, followed by brisk hand rubbing.
6. Iodine liniments are useful for reducing enlargements.
7. Dry pressure bandages, applied after hand rubbing, are very effective.

BOG SPAVIN

Distention of the capsule of the true hock joint, i.e., the joint between the tibia and the astragalus. Puffy swelling appears on the inside and a little to the front of the hock.

Causes:
1. Straight hocks.
2. Undue strain being thrown on hocks, e.g., slipping backwards, or overwork.

161

Symptoms:

1. Small bulges are seen on the inside of the hock.
2. Swelling is usually cold, painless and fluctuating.
3. Horse is usually not lame, unless swelling is sufficiently large to interfere with the action of the joint.
4. If case is recent and acute there will be inflammation, with attendant heat, swelling and pain—i.e., lameness.
5. If lameness is present horse will carry his leg and swing it clear of the ground.

Treatment:

1. If swelling is small and no lameness is present, no treatment is necessary.
2. To relax the joint a high-heeled (long, sloping wedge heels, not calkins) shoe may be applied. Shoe should be rolled at the toe and have very strong clip.
3. In acute cases, cold applications with astringent lotions are indicated. Massage will also help.
4. In chronic cases, after inflammation has subsided, blistering or firing may be tried. Acid firing is the safest and most likely to assist.

THOROUGH-PIN

Distension of the tendon sheath immediately above and on either side of the point of hock. Seldom causes lameness but is a technical unsoundness.

Causes:

1. Straight hocks.
2. Pulling up suddenly from a gallop—especially in soft going.
3. Rearing or kicking violently.

Symptoms:

1. If recent, and due to injury, swelling will be hot, tense and painful.
2. Usually, the swelling is cold, and not tender to the touch.
3. Swelling is egg-shaped, and often goes through from one side to the other. Is usually particularly evident on the inner side of the hock.

Treatment:

1. If Thorough-pin is small, no treatment is necessary. Work may continue.
2. If Thorough-pin is large, rest horse and apply a blister, or iodine ointment.
3. In acute cases, application of cooling, astringent lotion, followed by carefully applied pressure bandages, often are successful in reducing the swellings.
4. Some good results have been obtained by aspiration of the fluid and injection of Hydrocortisone into the sac. This should be left to the veterinary surgeon.
5. In chronic cases, acid firing may be resorted to.

WIND GALLS

Swellings just above the fetlock and on either side of it. Seldom give rise to lameness, except when associated with a sprain. Not a technical unsoundness.

Causes:

1. Strain and overwork.
2. Toe of hoof being allowed to get too long, and heels too low.

Treatment:

1. Treat as for Thorough-pin.
2. Hosing with cold water, or standing horse in running stream may help.
3. Shoe with wedge-heeled shoe to relieve pressure.
4. Pressure bandages in the stable are useful, but once used they become a permanent necessity.

CAPPED KNEE

Swelling of the tendon sheath which passes over the front of the knee (extensor tendon).

Causes:

1. Usually caused by a blow.

Treatment

1. Rest.
2. Massage—iodine liniment often useful.
3. Pressure.
4. If necessary, a mild blister may be applied.
5. Condition is usually of little consequence and does not result in lameness.

SORE SHINS

Inflammation of the metacarpal (cannon) bone. Occasionally also affects the corresponding bone in the hind leg. Occurs chiefly in young race horses.

Causes:
1. Strain—which causes inflammation of the periostium.

Symptoms:
1. Lameness—usually in both fore limbs, although possibly more pronounced in one limb.
2. Painful, diffuse swelling on front of cannon bone.
3. Loss of action in both fore limbs—tottery.
4. In older horses there is tenderness but often no swelling or heat.
5. Swelling eventually becomes thickened and more convex in shape.

Treatment:
1. Rest and laxative diet.
2. Apply warm fomentations or antiphlogistine or animalintex poultice.
3. After acute symptoms subside, apply iodine ointment.
4. After a rest it is advisable to blister affected area.

SESAMOIDITIS

Inflammation of the sesamoid bone and/or the sesamoid sheath of the flexor tendon.

Causes:
1. Pulling up suddenly.
2. Jumping—especially down a drop.
3. Faulty conformation—turned out toes.
4. Other causes—as for "sprained tendons"

Symptoms:
1. Lameness—usually well marked, but may be off and on.
2. Heat and usually swelling over the flexor tendons at the affected fetlock.
3. In serious cases, horse will not bring the heel to the ground.

Treatment:
1. Rest.
2. Cold water treatment.
3. Blister or pin fire, or acid fire.
4 No permanent cure.

CAPPED ELBOW

Sometimes termed a 'shoe boil'. An enlargement of the subcutaneous bursa at the point of the elbow.

Causes:

1. Lack of bedding—horse bruises point of elbow, either on the
   ground or with the heel of his shoe, when lying down.
2. May be caused by horse kicking forwards at flies in hot
   weather.

Symptoms:

1. A swelling appears at the elbow and extending on to the arm.
2. In the early stages, swelling may be painful on manipulation.
3. Limb may be stiff and movement hampered.
4. After about two weeks swelling, which was soft, becomes
   firm.

Treatment:

1. In early stages—cold water applications, followed by massage
   with astringent lotions.

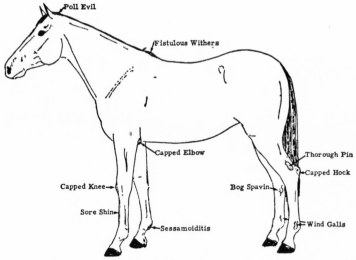

2. If swelling continues to increase in size, it may have to be
   drained. This is a job for the veterinary surgeon.

Preventive Measures:

1. Ensure horse has plenty of bedding—preferably tan, or wood
   shavings which will not be easily displaced.
2. If horse lies down frequently and is liable to injury (and in

early stages of capped elbow to avoid re-bruising swelling) fit 'stuffed sausage boot' (also called 'shoe boil boot').

3. Shoes should be sloped off very obliquely at heels. Heels kept well rounded. Or fit grass tips.

CAPPED HOCK

Bruising and subsequent swelling of the subcutaneous bursa at the point of the hock.

Causes:

1. Blows and kicks—usually self-inflicted.
2. Once an enlargement occurs on the point of the hock it is constantly bruised when the horse lies down.
3. Occasionally the swelling is due to thickening of the tendon. If the tendon is involved the swelling is hard—if it is the bursa, the swelling is soft. Thickening of the tendon is more serious and may cause lameness, but it is a rare condition.

Symptoms:

1. As in 'capped elbow', subcutaneous bursa is bruised and a soft swelling results.
2. If recent, swelling will be hot and painful to the touch.

Treatment:

1. Give plenty of bedding.
2. In recent cases cold applications should be used.
3. Antiphlogistine poultice, or a paste made of whitening and vinegar may reduce swelling if recent.
4. Repeated, mild, blistering is useful.

Preventive Measures:

1. Give plenty of bedding—as for capped elbow.
2. Pad sides of loose box.
3. Leave a light burning at night.
4. Fit hock boots as protection in stable and when travelling.

FISTULOUS WOUNDS

POLL EVIL

Soft, painful swelling on the top of the head, just behind the ears.

Causes:

1. Direct injury—i.e., a blow either self-inflicted (striking the poll against a manger, low doorway, etc.), or by someone striking the horse on the head with a whip handle, etc.

2. Pressure—heavy bridle or tight head collar.

3. May appear without any apparent cause.

Treatment:

1. Remove the cause (if caused by pressure).

2. Treatment is the same as for acute abscess, but securing drainage is difficult owing to site of injury.

3. In time the inflammatory fibrous growth which follows the initial swelling, goes deep and involves a portion of the ligamentum nuchæ—the largest ligament in the body—and causes intense pain during any movement of the head.

4. Keep horse in loose box and place food where horse can reach it with minimum head movement. Give laxative diet.

5. Poultice the region of the poll—antiphlogistine.

6. Most cases require surgical treatment—call the veterinary surgeon.

FISTULOUS WITHERS

Similar to Poll Evil but in this case the sinus is located in the region of the withers.

Causes:

1. Pressure and pinching from saddle or badly fitting harness.

2. May be a sequel to a sitfast.

Symptoms:

1. At first a small swelling appears on top of, or to either side of, the withers.

2. Swelling is sore and tender on manipulation.

3. The tissue under the skin is bruised and in time an abscess forms.

4. Horses in poor condition, or with high withers, are most liable to injury.

Treatment:

1. Same as for poll evil.

2. Like Poll Evil, Fistulous Withers is a very serious condition. Veterinary advice should be sought as early as possible. Neglected cases may be impossible to cure.

BIBLIOGRAPHY

Veterinary Notes for Horse Owners, M. Horace Hayes, pp. 377-385, 451, 456-458, and 475-477.

Practical Farriery—a Guide for Apprentices and Junior Craftsmen, C. Richardson, Pitman, pp. 27-30.

First Aid Hints for the Horse Owner, W. E. Lyon, pp. 55, 60-63, 65-66 and 77-78.

Horsemen's Veterinary Adviser, Joseph B. Davidson, pp. 46-50, 103-108, 190 and 195-199.

CHAPTER 25

WOUNDS

TYPES OF ACCIDENTAL WOUNDS

1. *Incised or Clean Cut Wounds:*
   Caused by a sharp cutting edge—knife, razor, glass. Not very common. The divided surfaces are smooth and regular. Bleeding is usually severe. Healing is favoured by the absence of bruising or tearing of the flesh.
2. *Lacerated or Torn Wounds:*
   Caused by blunt instruments entering the flesh and being forcibly torn out, i.e., barbed wire, projecting nail. Torn wounds are common. The broken surfaces are rough but bleeding is less than in an incised wound.
3. *Contused or Bruised Wounds:*
   Caused by blows, kicks, falls, galls, etc. The skin is not actually broken but the vessels under the skin are ruptured and the injured parts become infiltrated with blood. Relatively common.
4. *Puncture Wounds:*
   Caused by thorns, stakes, nails (in the feet), or stable forks (in the limbs). Usually such wounds have a small entrance but they may penetrate deep into the tissues. Punctured wounds are always serious. If in the foot, an abscess often forms. Unlike other wounds, where early closure is essential, punctured wounds must be kept open in order to drain. If allowed to close too soon, dirt may be trapped inside.

TREATMENT OF WOUNDS

1. *Stop the Bleeding*
   (a) If only small vessels are involved, exposure to the air will generally suffice. If not, the edges of the wound should be brought together with gentle pressure, or copiously irrigated with clean, cold water.
   (b) If wound involves arterial bleeding (blood is bright red and comes in spurts) a tourniquet may have to be applied. Apply tourniquet between the wound and the heart. Do not leave tourniquet on too long, loosen at regular intervals, or serious interference with the blood supply to the limb will result.

(c) If blood is venous (darker colour, steady flow) cold water should be sufficient. If it is not and pressure must be applied, apply pressure away from the heart.

2. *Clean Wound Thoroughly*

   (a) Clip away hair in vicinity of wound.
   (b) Wash thoroughly. Trickle constant stream of water very gently on the wound for fifteen minutes. Use hosepipe if available. Otherwise salt and water and cotton wool may be used. Avoid sponges and disinfectants.
   (c) Remove any foreign matter but do not probe.
   (d) If wound is a puncture, the veterinary surgeon must gently probe it but no unqualified person should try. If wound is near joint, there is danger of rupturing the joint oil sac.

3. *Dress the Wound*

   (a) Render broken surfaces antiseptic.
   (b) If wound is small, simply cover liberally with antibiotic wound powder.
   (c) Bring divided parts together as closely as possible and keep them in that position. If wound is large, sutures may be necessary.
   (d) Prevent movement of the injured part so far as possible.
   (e) Protect from flies. Bandaging is not always necessary but if a bandage is used the wound should be covered with surgical lint and then bandaged lightly—to allow room for any subsequent swelling.

4. *Additional Measures*

   (a) Give anti-tetanus injection. If horse has permanent anti-tetanus protection, give booster.
   (b) Keep loose box, or stall, scrupulously clean to avoid possible reinfection.
   (c) Rest horse and put on a laxative diet.
   (d) Avoid raising a dust when a wound is exposed.
   (e) If swelling is excessive, hot fomentations may be necessary.
   (f) Antibiotics—penicillin, streptomycin, etc.—have superseded disinfectants. Antibiotic treatment should always be given in cases of puncture wounds, near joints, into tendon sheaths and in the foot.

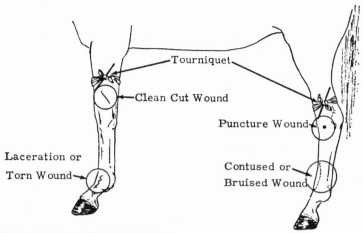

Tourniquet

Clean Cut Wound

Puncture Wound

Laceration or
Torn Wound

Contused or
Bruised Wound

SOME COMMON WOUNDS

1. *Bit Injuries*
   (a) Show on bars of mouths, tongue, cheeks, or in chin groove.
   (b) Causes—badly-fitting or worn bit, rough hands, ragged molars.
   (c) Treatment—discontinue work for a few days. After feeding, wash out mouth with warm water and salt. Remove cause—adjust bit.

2. *Girth Galls*
   (a) Show on soft skin behind the elbow.
   (b) Caused by too tight, too hard, or too loose girth on horse in soft condition.
   (c) Treatment—do not use saddle for a few days. Then use a Balding or a Mohair or string girth or encase girth in lamb's wool or inner tube.
   (d) Harden skin by applying salt and water, or methylated spirit, or witch hazel, several times a day.
   (e) In severe cases inflammation can be reduced by applying a cortisone ointment.

3. *Saddle Sore and Sore Back*
   (a) Any injury—from slight rub to severe swelling—caused by friction or pressure from badly fitting saddle.
   (b) Stop work under saddle. Exercise in hand.
   (c) Treat open wounds by fomentation or with kaolin paste.
   (d) Later harden with salt and water or methylated spirit.
   (e) Trace and remove cause of injury.

4. *Broken Knees*

(a) Injury to the surface of one or both knees caused by stumbling and falling. Varies from slight abrasion to exposure of the knee bones in severity.

(b) Any injury to a joint is a job for the veterinary surgeon.

(c) Treatment—complete rest. Irrigate continuously with cold water. Do not probe wound.

(d) With an open joint, the main danger is inflammation which may result in disease of the bone. An exostosis is formed, resulting in a permanently stiff joint.

(e) Protect the wound by putting on a knee-cap lined with clean surgical lint. Do not bandage the knee.

ANTISEPTICS

Most antiseptics retard healing by killing healing cells as well as harmful organisms.

Safe Antiseptics:

1. Saline solution (salt and water—1 teaspoon salt to 1 pint of water).
2. Potassium permanganate—enough just to turn the water purple.
3. Hydrogen Peroxide.
4. If using any other antiseptic on wounds, use in a very dilute solution (usually just one or two drops to a pint of water).
5. When disinfecting surgical equipment, use a strong solution of disinfectant.
6. Sulphanilamide is a good wound dressing.
7. Penicillin and other antibiotics, used under the guidance of a veterinary surgeon, are excellent and now generally replace disinfectants.
8. Some horses suffer allergic reactions to antibiotics and to some antiseptics. Watch all treated animals carefully.

BIBLIOGRAPHY

Veterinary Notes for Horse Owners, M. Horace Hayes, pp. 352-362.

First Aid Hints for the Horse Owner, W. E. Lyon, pp. 70-76 and 79.

Horsemen's Veterinary Adviser, Joseph B. Davidson, pp. 69-72 and 168-173.

Manual of Horsemanship, British Horse Society, pp. 226-232.

CHAPTER 26

WARBLES AND BOTS

WARBLES

Warble flies lay their eggs from May to August—chiefly on the horse's legs. In four to five days maggots hatch and bore through the skin. They wander through the system and by the following January to May they begin to appear as small lumps just under the skin, generally on the horse's back.

Here they grow much larger. Each maggot lies in a small swelling and feeds on the fluid exuded from the inflamed flesh. When the barrel-shaped maggot reaches maturity, it works its way out through a hole it makes in the skin, and falls to the grounds. Six weeks later the warble fly emerges.

Treatment

1. Warbles discovered which are not under the saddle or harness should be left alone to ripen naturally.
2. If warble is under the saddle, the saddle must be left off until the warbles have been removed.
3. Encourage warble to ripen by application of heat — hot fomentations or poultice.
4. When ripe, a small hole can be felt in the centre of the lump. The maggot can be squeezed out by gentle pressure of the thumbs at the base of the lump.
5. Do not press with thumbs until maggot is ready to emerge. There is a danger of bursting it under the skin and turning the lump septic.
6. After the warble has been squeezed out, or broken out of its own accord, wash out the cavity with dilute disinfectant and dress with iodine.

BOTS

These are the larvæ of gadflies. The gadfly, a brownish-yellow, hairy fly, about two-thirds of an inch long, lays its eggs during late summer and autumn on the skin of horses. The little yellow eggs are attached to the hairs, generally on the front parts of the horse, in reach of the tongue.

The eggs hatch in 10 to 14 days and the horse licks them off his coat and takes them into his mouth, where they penetrate the mucous membrane of the gums, lips and tongue. They remain there for a short growing period and later pass on to the stomach.

173

Symptoms:

1. If present in large quantities, there may be loss of condition —dry staring coat.
2. May be a rise in temperature and quickened pulse rate.
3. Horse may become restless and kick at belly.
4. Bots have differing effects on digestive system, horse may have intermittent diarrhoea or be constipated.
5. The presence of larvæ in the stomach has an inflammatory effect. The stomach wall rises and swells around the bots.
6. Bot larva are about three-quarters of an inch long and may be expelled in the dung, usually in the spring.
7. In small quantities, they are not injurious.

Prevention:

1. Keep horses away from pastureland during season when gadfly lays its eggs.
2. Pick, or clip, the eggs off the skin when seen.
3. Frequent grooming removes some eggs.
4. Weekly application of a 2% carbolic dip to those parts of the horse on which eggs are deposited destroys them.
5. When the eggs are found in quantity on the legs rub them over with a cloth dipped in kerosene.
6. Provide darkened shelters for horses at pasture during the gadfly season. This will give horses protection against the attacks of the flies.

Treatment:

1. Administer carbon bisulphide, or carbon tetrachloride by stomach tube. (Best done in early spring when larvæ are in stomach and before they pass out of horse.)
2. Animals should also be treated in the autumn, after the flies have disappeared. Drench with 2 tablespoons turpentine to 1 pint linseed oil.
3. Other modern treatments are available and treatment is best left to the veterinary surgeon along with a general programme of parasite control.

BIBLIOGRAPHY

Veterinary Notes for Horse Owners, M. Horace Hayes, pp. 272-276.

First Aid Hints for the Horse Owner, W. E. Lyon, pp. 88 and 103-104.

Manual of Horsemanship, British Horse Society, p. 245.

CHAPTER 27

LOSS OF CONDITION

OBVIOUS REASONS FOR LOSS OF CONDITION

1. Improper feeding.
2. Excessive work.
3. Lack of water.

LESS OBVIOUS REASONS FOR LOSS OF CONDITION

1. Worms.
2. Teeth.
3. Lampas.
4. Quidding.
5. Bolting food.
6. Parasites.
7. Stable vices.

INTESTINAL PARASITES

Various types of these parasites affect horses.
1. *Stomach Bots*—described in previous chapter.
2. *Common Intestinal or Round Worm*—stiff, white, and up to one foot in length. Generally about as thick as a pencil.

Symptoms:
   (a) In small quantities rarely gives rise to any symptoms.
   (b) In large numbers, may cause loss of condition, stoppage or irregularity of the bowels, and intermittent colic.

Treatment:
Treat with Piperazine. Best administered by veterinary surgeon using stomach tube. If horse is at pasture, change pasture after worming.
3. *Whip Worms*—about one and three-quarters inches long, very thin, occur in the rectum.
Symptoms:
   (a) Horse will rub his tail.
   (b) Sticky discharge will be visible at the anus.

Treatment:

(a) Piperazine is now generally used.

(b) Efficacy of piperazine is believed to be increased if a saline enema is given within about 24 hours.

(c) Saline enema—handful of salt in half a gallon of luke-warm water.

(d) Repeat treatment in three to four weeks (treatment is not very effective against immature worms).

4. *Red Worms*—also known as Large Strongyle, and Blood Worms. The most harmful of all parasites. Up to half an inch long and appears reddish in colour due to the blood it sucks. The larval forms may damage blood vessels and other organs.

Symptoms:

(a) May be very severe, especially in young horses.

(b) Loss of flesh.

(c) Anæmia.

(d) Hollow flanks.

(e) Dropped belly.

(f) Dry coat.

(g) Irregular bowel movements, occasionally diarrhoea.

(h) Worms may be visible upon careful examination of droppings.

(i) If in doubt, send sample of dung to veterinary surgeon for egg count.

(j) If left untreated, horse will suffer excessive debility and eventually be unable to rise.

Treatment:

(a) Phenothiazine or Thiabenzole—give as directed.

(b) Administer regularly throughout the year—usually every twelve to sixteen weeks. Follow the advice of veterinary surgeon.

(c) Regular 'worm count' should be done on each horse to ensure effectiveness of treatment.

Control of Red Worms:

(a) Pay particular attention to animals at grass, mares, foals and young stock.

(b) Dose all animals regularly.

(c) Avoid overstocking pastures.

(d) Mixed grazing is preferable to grazing horses only. Only equines are affected with red worm. Other animals will be able to destroy the eggs and larvæ.

(e) Clean pastures by either (i) ploughing up and cropping for a year or two with a straw crop. Re-sow with a three year ley. (ii) shut up pastures in turn and crop for hay. Two crops a year may be taken.

(f) Remove droppings regularly from paddocks (must be done within 24-48 hours to be effective).

(g) Allow dung-heap to rot thoroughly before ploughing-in or spreading as top dressing. Heat of fermentation kills eggs and larvæ.

TEETH

Molars

1. Upper molars grow downward and outward.

2. Lower molars grow upward and inward.

3. Therefore, the outside of the upper molars and the inside of the lower molars get uneven wear. They grow sharp and lacerate the cheeks and tongue.

4. Pain stops horse from eating normal amount of food. Also prevents him from chewing food.

5. Teeth should be floated (rasped) periodically. Generally once a year is sufficient.

6. Bad or decaying tooth may also stop horse from eating or chewing properly. Horse will probably hold his head on one side.

7. Check teeth regularly.

Lampas

1. Congestion of the blood vessels in the palate.

2. Gives a 'dropped' appearance to the mouth.

3. In young horses, usually associated with cutting of permanent teeth.

4. In old horses caused by sharp molars, indigestion, blood disorders and bit injuries.

Treatment:

(a) Inspect molars—rasp if necessary.
(b) Put horse on laxative diet.
(c) Give a course of Epsom salts in drinking water or food for about eight days. Or drench (two ounces for two to three days). Improves condition of the blood.
(d) Apply astringent lotion (e.g., witch hazel or alum, in 2% solution) to the palate three times a day.
(e) Rest horse for a few days and allow only soft foods.

Quidding

The food, after partial mastication, is rolled and shifted in the mouth and finally ejected.

Causes:

(a) Dental irregularities which cause pain when horse tries to chew.
(b) May be associated with 'sore throat'.
(c) Lampas.
(d) Some acrid substance in food.

Treatment:

Remove the cause.

Bolting Food

Horse swallows food without proper mastication.

Causes:

(a) Lampas.
(b) Dental irregularities—sharp teeth.
(c) Parasites.
(d) Stable vices.
(e) Greed.

Treatment:

(a) In first three cases—remove cause.
(b) If cause is greed, it is usually greed for corn. Add chaff, bran, horse cubes, etc., in higher proportion to grain.
(c) Put bar across manger.
(d) Feed from the ground.
(e) Put salt block in manger.

RINGWORM

Contageous skin disease caused by a fungus. Easily transmitted from one animal to another by saddlery, grooming kit, or by occupying the same loose box or stall as an affected horse.

Causes:

1. Contagion—from strange stable, during transportation, pre-infected clothing, tack or grooming kit.
2. Dirty horses more prone to attack.
3. Horses in low condition also prone to attack.
4. Inferior forage—musty hay and oats—may be cause of transmitting the disease round the stable.
5. Horses are more prone to ringworm in very cold weather.

Symptoms:

1. Raised, circular patches of hair on neck and shoulders.
2. Patches grow in size and scab off leaving greyish white crusts on the bare skin.
3. Spreads rapidly. Horse loses condition.

Treatment:

1. Isolate. Pay strict attention to disinfection of tack and grooming kit. Keep separate tack cleaning materials for the infected horse.
2. If coat is long, clip horse. Burn hair at once. Disinfect clippers after use.
3. Wash actual ringworm patches with a warm solution of washing soda, scraping off each scab.
4. Apply Iodine, or Blue Mercury Ointment, or Iodoform Ointment carefully to each patch, working in thoroughly.
5. Keep horse well groomed and disinfect kit often. After grooming, go over horse with stable rubber damped with a mild disinfectant.
6. Burn all litter and disinfect loose box thoroughly.
7. Wear overalls when grooming infected horse. Keep sleeves rolled down and wear rubber gloves, or wash hands thoroughly afterwards. Ringworm can be passed from the horse to his attendant.
8. Thoroughness in treating all ringworm patches is vital. The disease will spread if just one spot is neglected. Repeat treatment of all spots until they appear dead.

9. Successful treatment of ringworm requires skilled veterinary attention. Treatments are constantly changing and the veterinary surgeon will advise the most up to date and effective treatment.
10. Keep horse isolated and under observation for some time, in case of further outbreak.

CANADIAN POX

Very similar to ringworm in appearance, but eruption usually in clusters of pimples, most frequently near the girth or behind the elbow. Highly contagious disease due to a bacillus.

Treatment:
1. As for ringworm.
2. After treating the sores with iodine (or a solution of one part carbolic acid to 40 parts water) apply Boracic Acid and flour —or other dressing recommended by veterinary surgeon.
3. Put horse on laxative diet.
4. Precautions should be taken as for ringworm to avoid spread of the disease, both to other horses and to attendant.

ACNE

Skin eruption similar to Canadian Pox but the pimples are scattered and do not occur in clusters. Generally occurs near the withers. Much less common than Canadian Pox.

Treatment:
Same as Canadian Pox.

MANGE

There are three main types of mange parasites:
Sarcoptic: Most serious—now rare. Caused by a burrowing mite. The parasite generally attacks near the withers but is harboured in infected harness and often also attacks the face.
2. *Soroptic:* Similar to sarcoptic but less serious. In this case the mite does not burrow but is a scavenger upon the skin surface (Caused by a different mite.) Seeks the cover of long hair and most often found in the mane and tail.
3. *Symbiotic:* Caused by a different mite again and is confined to the legs and heels—especially in horses with a lot of 'feather'.

Symptoms:
1. Itchiness.
2. In Symbiotic mange, stamping of feet, often rapidly repeated.
3. Affected parts become thicker and wrinkled and hair eventually falls off leaving skin covered with a thin crust.

Causes:
1. Contagion.
2. Dirt and lack of grooming.

Treatment:
1. Isolation.
2. Put on laxative diet.

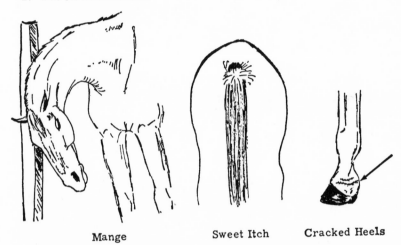

| Mange | Sweet Itch | Cracked Heels |

3. Clip and burn all hair.
4. There are many new parasiticides, which give better control than old remedies containing sulphur, which itself may cause dermatitis. Treat as instructed by the veterinary surgeon.
5. Precautions must be taken to kill all parasites sheltering outside the body. Otherwise re-infection will occur. Use a blow lamp to kill parasites sheltering in woodwork, etc.

TICKS
Similar to those found on dogs.

Treatment:
1. Search out ticks and dab with mineral oil, or turpentine.
2. When they relax their hold, they will fall off or can be snipped off with scissors.
3. Do not simply pull off or they will make a small wound on the skin where they were clinging.

LICE

Found on horses in poor condition. Also picked up by horses at grass. They are blood-sucking and soon pull horse down in condition.

Symptoms:

1. Give blotchy appearance to the coat.

2. Itchiness—horse will rub against any convenient object.

3. Lice and nits (eggs) can be seen on close examination.

Treatment:

1. Clip horse and groom thoroughly.

2. Apply a Derris Root or D.D.T. preparation—e.g., Pulvex.

3. Repeat treatment in ten days to catch the eggs which have hatched since first application.

4. Disinfectants are useless against lice. They only blister tne skin.

BIBLIOGRAPHY

Veterinary Notes for Horse Owners, M. Horace Hayes, pp. 14, 30, 33, 170-174, 176-177 and 276-284.

First Aid Hints for the Horse Owner, W. E. Lyon, pp. 103-105, 107-108 and 81-84.

Your Horse, A Veterinary Book, Sporting Life Publication, pp. 143-145.

Horsemen's Veterinary Adviser, Joseph B. Davidson, pp. 80-83 and 144-149.

CHAPTER 28

NON-PARASITIC SKIN DISEASES

CRACKED HEELS

Cracks in the heel region, running crossways, sometimes extending from one side of the heel to the other.

Causes:

1. Exposure to wet and cold.
2. Irritation from mud.
3. Injuries from ropes and hobbles.
4. Bad stable management (standing in dirty, wet bedding; ammonia fumes aggravate the condition).
5. Washing horse's legs and failing to dry properly. This removes natural oils which keep skin supple, and makes horse prone to chill.
6. Sweat running down the legs to the heels (common in race horses).

Symptoms:

1. Skin in the hollow of the pastern on one or more legs becomes tender, reddened and scaly.
2. Small vesicles form and then rupture, causing a crack over the point where vesicle developed.
3. If not treated, crack extends and deepens, its edges becoming thickened and calloused.
4. Horse is lame—goes on toes. May improve with exercise.
5. Limb may become swollen.

Treatment

1. Wash with warm water and medicated soap. Dry thoroughly.
2. Clip off all hair in hollow of pastern.
3. In mild cases, in the early stages, apply zinc and caster oil ointment.
4. In advanced cases it may be necessary to dress wounds with sulphanilamide pads and bandage to restrict movement.
5. Veterinary advice should be sought. A course of antibiotics is very useful. Rest, laxative diet.
6. When healing starts, keep heels soft with Vaseline.

1. If possible, do not clip legs. Hair protects them.
2. Do not wash muddy legs. Bandage lightly (over straw) until dry and then brush off mud.
3. If legs are washed, always dry carefully.
4. In wet, muddy country, oil heels, or apply Vaseline, before taking horse out.
5. Keep legs warm at night with stable bandages.

MUD FEVER

Similar to cracked heels, but also affects the inner side of the forelimbs, and the front of the hind legs from fetlock upwards.

Causes:

1. Similar to cracked heels. Washing legs is a prime cause.

Symptoms:

1. Limbs swell, heat and tenderness of the skin.
2. Skin becomes thickened, rough, and covered with little scabs.
3. When scabs are detached, hair falls off with them and a red base is exposed.
4. Lameness, depending on degree of the disease.

Treatment:

1. If there is a fever present, give mild dose of Epsom Salts in horse's water or in bran mash. Use quarter of a pound of Epsom Salts.
2. Keep horse on laxative diet, and rest.
3. Wash legs with warm water, rinse and dry thoroughly.
4. Apply an astringent lotion, or zinc ointment, or medication provided by veterinary surgeon.

Prevention:

1. As for cracked heels.
2. Do not wash mud off—allow it to dry and then brush it off.

NETTLERASH (Urticaria, Hives)

A skin disorder in which round swellings appear on various parts of the body.

Causes:

1. Sudden change in diet. Error of diet—i.e., too much grain, too little work. Overheated blood.
2. Occurs most frequently in young animals.
3. Often seen when young animals are first turned out on to lush pasture.

Symptoms:

1. Round lumps appear very suddenly on the body. Vary in size from very small to several inches across.
2. Swellings are flat on the surface and elastic on manipulation.
3. Rarely is there any irritation.
4. In mild cases, lumps may appear on the neck only. Otherwise they occur either in patches, or all over the body.

Treatment:

1. Keep horse at rest in loose box. Laxative diet.
2. An antihistamine should be administered, and dose repeated for two days. Call veterinary surgeon.
3. Swellings may be dressed with a cooling lotion (lead or calamine) if they persist.
4. Swellings usually disappear spontaneously.

SWEET ITCH (mane and tail eczema)

Skin disease, probably due to an allergic reaction to some pasture plant, found mainly in small ponies. Also affects other classes of horses, and most common when they are at pasture and grass is plentiful. Seasonal—liable to recur annually in spring and summer.

Causes:

1. Most probably an allergic reaction to some plant.
2. Wet weather may cause maceration of skin and facilitate entrance of infection.
3. Horses and ponies in fat condition seem especially prone to sweet itch.

Symptoms:

1. Areas of skin at root of mane, tail and on the neck and withers, become thickened, inflamed and scaly.
2. Animal rubs against any convenient object.
3. Upper layer of skin is damaged and serum leaks out and collects on surface.

4. The hair falls out leaving moist, bare patches.

5. Later, the skin becomes thickened, hard, wrinkled and scaly.

Treatment:

1. As Sweet Itch is thought to be an allergic response to some component of grass—green food should be withheld.

2. Clip hair from affected parts.

3. Wash with warm water and mercurial soap. Dry well.

4. Apply astringent ointment, or dressing—e.g., zinc and sulphur ointment, or sulphur and tar, or salicyclic acid ointment, or propamidine cream.

5. In addition to local treatment—treat with antihistamine injection repeated at three to four day intervals.

6. Some degree of prevention can be achieved by limiting the intake of fresh, young grass at the time of seasonal occurrance.

6. A daily dose of Epsom Salts in drinking water or in feed is helpful.

7. Feed no grain—hay may be fed together with bran or linseed mashes.

BIBLIOGRAPHY

Veterinary Notes for Horse Owners, M. Horace Hayes, pp. 177-179 and 183-186.

First Aid Hints for the Horse Owner, Lt.-Col. W. E. Lyon, pp. 85-87.

Manual of Horsemanship, British Horse Society, pp. 232 and 244.

Horsemen's Veterinary Adviser, Joseph B. Davidson, pp. 150-151.

CHAPTER 29

INTERNAL DISEASES

THE LYMPHATIC SYSTEM

1. An extensive system of vessels and their associated glands, widely distributed throughout the body, which play an important role in the body.
2. Lymph vessels may be compared to the system of blood vessels throughout the body, but instead of containing blood, they contain a fluid called lymph.
3. Unlike blood vessels, the lymph vessels do not form a complete circle.
4. Lymph vessels begin in the extremities and the organs as a system of thin-walled capillaries with blind endings.
5. Lymph capillaries collect together to form larger vessels. The larger vessels have valves to prevent flow of lymph backwards towards blind-ending capillaries.
6. Lymphatic vessels eventually collect and flow into the large veins close to the heart.
7. Before entering the bloodstream, all lymph passes through one or more lymph nodes (or glands).
8. There is a continuous flow of lymph, just as there is a continuous flow of blood. Having no special organ, like the heart, to drive the flow, the lymphatic flow is maintained by movement of the surrounding parts, e.g., muscles, tendons, etc. These massage the fluid along the vessels.
9. The purposes of the lymph stream are:
   (a) To keep in balance the amount of salts and protein in the tissue spaces within the body.
   (b) To maintain a proper fluid balance within the body.
10. There is a continuous flow of fluid from the blood stream into the tissue spaces and from the tissue spaces into the lymph stream or back to the blood stream.
11. Lymph is a colourless or yellowish fluid.
12. The lymph nodes act as a filter to the lymph stream.
13. Many conditions and diseases are associated with the lymphatic system: e.g., "filled legs" which subsequently "walk down" are due to tissue-spaces which are over filled with fluid, and its subsequent dispersal by muscular activity which speeds up the flow of lymph.

LYMPHANGITIS (Monday Morning Disease)

Constitutional blood disorder causing inflammation of the lymphatic system and glands. Most frequently affects a hind limb.

Causes:

1. Any factor which prevents the proper flow of lymph—particularly infection.
2. Bacteria entering through an infected wound in tne lower part of the limb may set up infection in the lymphatic system.
3. Lack of exercise, combined with the usual corn diet.
4. Over nutritious feeding.
5. Sudden changes of diet.

Symptoms:

1. Extreme lameness.
2. At onset of attack, quickened pulse, heavy breathing, and often a shivering fit.
3. A limb, or limbs (usually one or both the hind legs) become swollen, hot and painful.
4. The swelling may extend from foot to stifle. Leg may be twice normal size.
5. Due to pain, the leg is constantly moved and held up.

Treatment:

1. Horse should be put in a loose box and either led out or made to move round the box for a few minutes two or three times a day.
2. Put on laxative diet. Cut out all corn.
3. The old treatment was to give full dose of aloes in a ball. This practice still has something to recommend it and is sometimes followed.
4. Modern treatment is sulphonamide drugs and antibiotics in the early stages of an attack. Call the veterinary surgeon.
5. If no aloes ball has been given, add two to four oz. Epsom salts to feed or water two or three times daily.
6. Apply hot fomentations to swollen leg for one hour two or three times a day. Dry leg carefully afterwards.
7. Later, give walking exercise for ten minutes several times a day.
8. Turn horse out on sparse pasture to encourage him to move around and so reduce swelling.

Prevention:
1. Horses prone to attack should be exercised every day.
2. On the rest day, bran should be substituted for the grain ration, and quiet walking exercise should be given.
3. Recurrence of the disease may cause a permanent thickness of the leg.

STRANGLES

An acutely contagious disease caused by bacteria—a specific strangles streptococcus—which is inhaled and sets up catarrh of the upper air passages, and fever. The germ enters the lymphatic vessels and is caught in the lymph glands (usually those of the head and neck) where it breeds and eventually causes abscesses.

Symptoms:
1. Dullness and apathy.
2. Rise in temperature—to between 103° and 105°.
3. Mucous membrane of the eye changes from healthy light pink to an unhealthy red colour.
4. Thin watery discharge from one or both nostrils will turn to a thick yellowish discharge.
5. Sore throat and coughing.
6. The glands under the jaw will swell and become hot and tender.
7. The head is held stiffly extended. The horse has difficulty in swallowing.
8. After a few days an abscess forms and then bursts.
9. After the abscess breaks, the horse's temperature quickly falls.
10. Strangles most frequently attacks horses under six years of age.

Treatment:
1. Isolate horse in roomy, airy loose box with plenty of fresh air.
2. Carefully disinfect the old box and all clothing, saddlery and equipment which may have been in contact with the sick horse.
3. Keep horse warm with rugs and flannel bandages.
4. The strangles bacteria is killed by most antibiotics. Early diagnosis is important—to prevent spread of the disease—so call veterinary surgeon at earliest signs.
5. Give inhalations of eucalyptus.
6. Cleanse nostrils frequently with warm water and keep them smeared with eucalyptus ointment. Do not use even a weak solution of disinfectant in the nostrils. The membranes are extremely sensitive and disinfectant may aggravate the disease.

7. Encourage abscesses to mature by application of stimulating liniment, hot fomentations or poultices.
8. When abscess is mature (or pointing) it will burst, discharging a thick pus. If it does not burst it should be lanced by the veterinary surgeon.
9. After abscess bursts, destroy matter and treat as an ordinary wound.
10. Horse should be fed soft food—damp bran mash, boiled oats, etc. If food is not soft the horse will have difficulty eating due to sore throat.
11. Good nursing is essential. Strangles usually runs its course in six weeks.
12. Convalescence is long, from two to three months. An additional long period of conditioning is necessary before normal work can be resumed.

Prevention:
1. Strict stable management and hygiene, combined with fresh air, suitable food and adequate exercise help prevent occurrence of strangles.
2. Infection usually occurs from contaminated food, drinking water (drinking troughs), utensils, clothing or litter.
3. Infection sometimes occurs during transit, or while staying in strange stables. Ensure proper disinfection of all premises and equipment.
4. Avoid conditions favouring development — e.g., chills, debility, etc.

AZOTURIA ("Tying up")

A peculiar disease of horses which may be met in any type of animal at any time of year, especially horses in training for competitive events or hunting. It is a degenerative condition of muscle, especially over the loins and in the hind quarters.

Causes:
1. Exact cause not known. Disease always follows enforced idleness of horse in hard condition—particularly if grain ration is not reduced.
2. Accumulation of glycogen in the muscles of resting horse which, on sudden activity, is used up quickly creating a marked increase in production of lactic acid which causes swelling and degeneration of muscle fibres.

3. Deficiency of Vitamin C may be a cause.
4. Putting a horse straight back to hard work after an enforced period of rest.

Symptoms:

1. Horse goes out sound but later slackens and shows muscular stiffness.
2. Horse starts to stagger and roll in his gait. Shows marked lameness in a hind limb.
3. Profuse sweating, and quickened breathing.
4. Muscles over the loins may be seen quivering.
5. Horse may collapse if forced to proceed.
6. Temperature rises to about 103°.
7. Muscles over loins may become very hard and tense.
8. If urine is passed, it is coffee-coloured.

Treatment:

1. Get horse home and into loose box, if possible. Do not try to make him walk, transport him in a trailer or horse box.
2. Apply hot blankets to his loins.
3. Call the veterinary surgeon.
4. Mild cases recover quickly, but severe cases may be followed by death in a few days.
5. During recovery, keep horse on laxative, easily assimilated diet, i.e., bran mashes, gruel, green food and hay.

Prevention:

1. Sensible diet.
2. Whenever possible, give some exercise (if only turning into paddock) every day.
3. When horse is not worked, or if work is greatly reduced, adjust diet immediately.

TETANUS (Lock Jaw)

A disease caused by the tetanus bacillus which gets into the blood stream via a wound. The disease is more prevalent in some districts than others. Fatal in nine cases out of ten.

Symptoms:

1. Rise in temperature to 103° to 105°F.
2. General stiffening of the limbs.
3. Membrane of the eye will extend over eyeball.

191

4. Horse becomes highly nervous.
5. Horse stands with nose and tail stretched out, and as disease progresses, jaw becomes set.

Treatment:
1. Call veterinary surgeon immediately. If disease is seen in early stages, before jaw becomes set, there is a chance of recovery.
2. Keep horse absolutely quiet, in a dark box.
3. Feed only soft, laxative foods. Withhold hay, as it may cause choking.
4. Keep plenty of fresh water within easy reach.
5. Treatment consists of administering very large doses of concentrated tetanus antitoxin both intravenously and subcutaneously, every day until definite improvement sets in.
6. If infected wound can be found, treat with antiseptic.

Prevention:
1. All horses should be immunized against tetanus, and given annual booster shots.
2. If horse has not been immunized, or if in any doubt, anti-tetanus serum, which will give temporary immunity only, should be given as early as possible after any injury. Most dangerous injuries are puncture wounds, tetanus germs are destroyed by contact with the air, but thrive in deep, puncture wounds.

PNEUMONIA

Inflammation of the lungs (frequently following strangles, or influenza).

Causes:
1. Invasion by virulent organisms. Often following contagious disease such as strangles, glanders, influenza.
2. Colds or chills.
3. Long exposure or over exertion.
4. A drench going the 'wrong way', or a stomach pump entering the windpipe by mistake.

Symptoms:
1. Rapid, shallow breathing.
2. Dullness and loss of appetite.
3. High fever, accompanied by muscular weakness and staggering.
4. The head is outstretched, and the nostrils dilated.
5. A short, soft cough appears at times.

6. There is usually a scant, rusty-coloured nasal discharge. This later becomes greyish and more abundant.
7. The pulse is rapid but weak.
8. Horse will rarely lie down. He may have shivering attacks.
9. If disease progresses favourably, the temperature will gradually subside after seven or eight days. The horse appears brighter and feeds better.
10. Complete recovery takes place in two or three weeks.
11. In unfavourable cases, the breathing becomes more rapid and laboured. The pulse weakens and is irregular.
12. Any sudden drop in temperature is a bad sign.

Treatment:
1. Good nursing, combined with plenty of fresh air. Keep horse in loose box with rugs and stable bandages for warmth.
2. Antibiotics and sulphonamide drugs are given.
3. Give inhalations of eucalyptus or friar's balsam.
4. Take the chill off drinking water. Epsom salts may be put in drinking water to keep the bowels open.
5. Do not give purgatives (balls). Do not drench.
6. Mustard plasters applied to the chest relieve the respiratory distress.
7. Laxative diet—linseed tea, bran mashes, carrots, etc.
8. Pneumonia is a very serious illness—call the veterinary surgeon as soon as possible.

COLIC

A set of symptoms indicating abdominal pain.

Causes:
1. Too much food—over-taxing the stomach.
2. Unsuitable or unsuitably prepared foods—too much new green grass, new oats, mouldy hay, too much boiled grain.
3. Stoppage between the stomach and the small intestine.
4. Digestive trouble—bolting food, sudden change of diet.
5. Watering and working immediately after feeding. Watering when overheated.
6. Crib biting and wind sucking.
7. Sand in the stomach.
8. Parasites.
9. Twisted gut.
10. Stones in the kidneys or bladder.

Symptoms:
There are two types of Colic: Spasmodic and Flatulent.

Spasmodic
1. Pain is intermittent. It is due to spasmodic contractions of the muscular wall of the bowel arising most often from local irritation.
2. Spasms are usually violent.
3. Horse kicks at belly and paws the ground.
4. Horse may lie down and roll.
5. Horse may look round at his flanks, stamp, and break out in cold, patchy sweat.
6. Temperature does not rise at first but may do so later due to excitement as pain becomes more frequent and intervals of rest are shortened.
7. Breathing may become hurried and 'blowing'.
8. After a time the pain subsides and horse begins to feed and drink normally. But the symptoms may recur after an interval.

Flatulent (Wind Colic)
1. Due to obstruction of the bowel and fermentation of food and production of gases in bowel.
2. Symptoms are similar to those of spasmodic colic, but usually the pain is more continuous, and less severe.
3. Belly is inflated. Horse appears uneasy. He wanders round his loose box and may crouch but seldom lies down.

Twisted gut
A form of colic—may be caused by a stumble or fall or by too heavy a feed after strenuous work. It is sometimes thought to be caused by rolling—but equally it may cause rolling. In cases of twisted gut the temperature rises to 105°—higher than other forms of colic.

Treatment:
1. If outside, bring horse in to nearest stable and encourage him to stale.
2. Keep horse warm. Bed loose box down well. Horse may lie down but should be watched in order to avoid injury if he rolls.
3. Gentle walking exercise may be beneficial.
4. Give colic drink which has been previously made up by veterinary surgeon.

5. If no colic drink is available administer colic drink made of: 2 tablespoons turpentine, 1 pint linseed oil, 2 tablespoons of whisky or brandy.
6. Other remedies that can be used:
   1½ pints of heated beer, half a tumbler whisky or rum in 1½ pints warm water. Or, one teaspoon of ginger in half a pint of warm milk.
7. Hot blankets rolled up and applied to the belly underneath and well back will relieve pain and stimulate the bowels.
8. If the horse has not recovered within an hour, call the veterinary surgeon.

WHISTLING, ROARING AND BROKEN WIND

Whistling and roaring are different degrees of an affection of the larynx due to paralysis of the left vocal cord. Broken wind is a different disease affecting the lungs.

Whistling

A high pitched noise generally heard at fast paces. A whistler is generally better able to carry out hard work than a roarer, but whistling may lead to roaring.

Roaring

A deep noise heard on inspiration at fast paces. Horse may become so distressed at fast paces that he must be pulled up. May lead to heart trouble.

Causes of Whistling and Roaring:

1. Heredity—animals may not show symptoms until they are three or four years old or even later.
2. Strangles—insufficient recovery time given after an attack of strangles is commonly responsible for causing whistling and roaring.
3. May also follow an attack of pharyngitis, bronchitis, pneumonia, influenza or pleurisy.
4. May result from lead poisoning.

Symptoms:

1. Unless both sides of the larynx are paralysed, no abnormal sound is heard when the horse is at rest.
2. Whistling may be heard at trot, canter or gallop.
3. Roaring is usually heard in the faster paces, but is sometimes also heard at trot.

4. The sound in both cases may be scarcely perceptible or quite noticeable, according to the gravity of the case.
5. A fit horse will make less noise than an unfit one.

Treatment:
1. Tracheotomy—A tube inserted into the wind pipe, not too low down. Tubed horses make a lot of noise but suffer no distress. A tubed horse may drown if he falls in a ditch or river, carry a cork when hunting.
2. Ventricle stripping—this operation consists of stripping the lining membrane from the pouch behind the vocal cord and allowing the cords to stick to the walls of the larynx. This leaves the air space permanently open. This operation, even if not always a complete success, makes a previously unsound horse workably sound.

Prevention:
1. Do not breed from affected horses.
2. Rest sufficiently after attacks of strangles, bronchitis, etc.

Broken Wind (Heaves)
Breakdown of the air vesicles of the lungs.

Causes:
1. Too much strain on lungs due to chronic cough, or after bronchitis, asthma, pleurisy or pneumonia.
2. Excessive feeding, particularly of bulky foods, before exercise.
3. Feeding dusty hay.
4. Over-galloping an unfit horse.

Symptoms:
1. Harsh, dry cough, gets worse with exercise.
2. Slight discharge from the nose.
3. Cough later becomes short and weak.
4. Breathing is laboured after any exertion.
5. Double effort at exhalation—watch flanks, horse appears to heave twice on breathing out.

Treatment:
1. Treatment is palliative, there is no cure for broken wind.
2. Special feeding can help keep horse in work, particularly in early stages.
3. All food should be damped. Linseed oil should be mixed with food three times a week.
4. Hay is best avoided and many horses are successfully fed prepared feed, containing grain and also sugar beet plup, fed wet, and pelleted grass or hay.

5. Some horses thrive best if kept outside.
6. Bed on shavings or peat to prevent horse eating too much bulk in form of straw.

HIGH BLOWING

Not an unsoundness. A noise made by horse during exhalation only. It is caused by an abnormality of the false nostril which vibrates as horse breathes out. Quite common among well-bred horses. High blowers are said to be very sound winded horses.

COLD IN THE HEAD

Similar to a cold in man, brought about by infection or exposure. Not serious in itself but serious complications may result if horse is worked with a cold.

Symptoms:
1. Sneezing. Horse is dull and lethargic.
2. Rise in temperature which may remain above normal for two or three days.
3. Thin nasal discharge. Later becomes thick.
4. Horse may have a cough.
5. Eyes may water.
6. Coat will be dull and staring.

Treatment:
1. Isolate to prevent spread.
2. Keep horse warmly clothed but allow plenty of fresh air.
3. Feed laxative diet.
4. Give inhalations of friar's balsam to assist discharge.
5. Give electuary to relieve cough.
6. Do not work the horse.

COUGHS

Coughs are symptoms of several troubles.

Causes:
1. Horse brought up from grass may cough due to impure air in the stable, or indigestion, or too sudden change from soft to hard food.
2. Sore throat—laryngitis.
3. Irritants—e.g., some of a drench going down the wind pipe instead of the gullet. Something stuck in the throat.

4. Indigestion. May be due to discomfort in stomach and intestines but if no improvement after removing any apparent cause, suspect worms.
5. Broken wind.
6. Teething.

Treatment:
1. Treatment consists of correct diagnosis and removal of the cause.
2. If due to coming up from grass—keep stable door open night and day to allow fresh air. Make change of food gradual.
3. In cases of Laryngitis, keep horse warm in well ventilated stable. Give inhalations of eucalyptus. Smear electuary on tongue frequently. Massage throat with liniment. Feed gruel, hay tea, grass, bran mashes.
4. Coughs due to irritants generally right themselves in a short time. If considerable amount of fluid gets into lungs the irritation may cause pneumonia.
5. Coughs due to indigestion—give 1½ pints linseed oil. If no improvement, have horse dosed for worms.
6. Teething cough will disappear as soon as the cause disappears. Feed laxative diet and add Epsom salts to food.

INFLUENZA

Highly infectious disease.

Causes:
1. Exact cause unknown but spread by contagion, clothing, food, bedding, grooming kit, infected stables.

Symptoms:
1. Two types: (a) Mild type — runs its course in six to eight days.
   (b) Severe type or pinkeye—most critical period is fifth to eighth day.
2. In both types — high temperature, 103° to 106°, and exhausted condition.
3. Catarrhal discharge from eyes and nostrils.
4. Coughing and great depression.
5. Severe type is recognised by bright red colour of the eye as opposed to yellowish colour in mild type.
6. In severe type, swellings may develop on legs, muzzle and belly.
7. Pneumonia may develop.

8. Severe type is often fatal. If cured there may be permament respiratory trouble.

Treatment:

1. Prevention is better than cure. Healthy horse is less liable to the disease than one in poor condition.
2. If an outbreak occurs in the stable, take the temperature of every horse before work. A rise in temperature is the earliest symptom of mild cases.
3. Good stable management, isolation of new horses, and care when travelling will help to prevent the disease.
4. If influenza occurs—isolate the patient at once.
5. Keep warm in airy, draught-free loose box. Bandage legs for extra warmth.
6. Careful nursing is vital. Feed soft food, little and often.
7. Steam head frequently with friar's balsam or eucalyptus.
8. Call the veterinary surgeon.

Prevention:

Horses can, and should, be immunized annually against the known influenza viruses prevalent in the district.

BIBLIOGRAPHY

Veterinary Notes for Horse Owners, H. Horace Hayes, pp. 45, 48-64, 90-101, 121-124, 129-130 and 132-133.

First Aid Hints for the Horse Owner, Lt.-Col. W. E. Lyon, pp. 69-70, 90-103, 107 and 112-115.

Your Horse, Sporting Life Publications, pp. 90-95, 109-112, 121-125, 129-141.

Horsemen's Veterinary Adviser, Joseph B. Davidson, pp. 52-54, 63-65, 130-131, 135-141.

Manual of Horsemanship, British Horse Society, pp. 238-240 and 242-243.

Top Form Book of Horse Care, Frederick Harper, pp. 139-142, 144 and 145-146.

GLOSSARY OF TERMS

ABSCESS

Localized collection of pus in a cavity made by disintegration of tissues in any organ or part of the body.

Chronic abscess—one which may have been in existence for some time.

Acute abscess—one which forms quickly and is often accompanied by pain.

ABSORBENT

Medicines which suck or draw off dead tissue in the system.

Vessels which absorb or take up various fluids of the body.

ACUTE

An ailment or disease with brief and severe symptoms which terminates in a few days with relief, cure or death.

ANAEMIA

A deficiency of the blood.

ASTRINGENTS

Medicines which restore the tone of muscular fibres and check morbid discharges by their power to contract muscular fibres and coagulate certain fluids.

BOG SPAVIN

A soft swelling on the inner front surface of the hock joint. It is caused by strain.

BONE SPAVIN

Bony enlargement on the inside, lower aspect of the hock.

CHRONIC

A disease of long duration (as opposed to acute).

CURB

Enlargement of the ligament or tendon just below the point of hock. Due to sudden strain.

CYST

A closed cavity containing either liquid or semi-solid secretions of the lining membrane.

SEROUS CYST

Inflammation of the skin covering a bony projection, i.e., capped hock.

DRENCH

Liquid medicine administered orally by means of a "Drenching Bottle".

EFFUSION

Out-pouring of the watery part of the blood through the walls of overloaded vessels.

EWE-NECKED

A neck which is concave from withers to poll instead of convex. An upside-down neck.

EXOSTOSIS

Abnormal deposit of bone.

FORELEGS OUT OF ONE HOLE

Very narrow chest. Little room for the lungs to function properly so horses with this conformation are usually non-stayers, often winded. Horses built this way will often hit themselves.

GOOD BONE

Cannon bone and tendons measuring $8\frac{1}{2}$ to 9 inches in circumference just below the knee. A horse with good bone will be better able to carry weight.

GOOSE RUMPED

Tail set on too low and quarters drooping away to the hocks.

HERRING GUTTED

Horse with barrel too narrow compared to legs—too much daylight underneath. Horse runs up light.

JUMPING BUMP

Pronounced point of croup.

LIGAMENTS

Bands of white (inelastic) and yellow (elastic) fibrous tissue. Ligaments hold tendons and joints in place—join bone to bone. Check ligaments join bone to deep flexor tendon (below knee) and (above knee) to the superficial flexor tendon.

MUCUS

Fluid substance secreted by the mucous membrane.

MUSCLE

Bundle or sheet of contractile fibres which produce movement in the animal body. Muscles are attached to bones by tendons or ligaments.

PUS

A liquid of creamy colour and consistency, secreted in sores or abscesses.

SHORT OF RIB

Horse with big gap between the last rib and the point of the hip. (Short back but long loin.)

SPLINTS
Bony enlargements which arise on the splint bone, the cannon bone or both.
TENDONS
Tough, white, inelastic cords which connect muscles to bones.
TUCKED UP
Refers to a horse whose belly goes up against the backbone. (Usually occurs after a hard day's work.)
WELL RIBBED UP
Rib cage extends well back, only room for a clenched fist between the last rib and the point of the hip.
VESICLES
Small blisters or vessels containing fluid.
WIND GALLS
Swelling of the synovial membrane of the fetlock joint (joint sac), or the sheath of the tendon. Caused by strain.

HUNTING TERMS

AWAY
When a fox leaves the covert he has "gone away". When hounds leave the covert on the line of a fox they are said to be "away".
BABBLE
If hounds give tongue on no scent or on a scent too faint to follow, or on a scent other than a fox, they are said to "babble".
BLANK
Failure to find a fox is "to draw blank".
BRUSH
A fox's tail.
BUTTON
The right to wear the hunt buttons and colours is a mark of distinction awarded to some regular supporters and followers by the Master.
BYE
A bye day is an extra hunting day, not scheduled on the fixture card.
CAP
1. Headgear worn by the Master and Hunt Staff.
2. A fee which visitors may be asked to pay.
3. A collection taken on one day for some particular purpose, i.e., charity, hunt fences, etc.

CAST

When hounds lose the line the huntsman may "cast" them (make a planned series of moves) in order to recover the scent. Hounds may also cast themselves.

CHECK

Hounds check when they lose the line of a fox.

COLOURS

A distinctive colour, usually of the collar on a scarlet coat, which distinguishes the uniform of one hunt from another. Some hunts have coats of another colour, not scarlet.

COUPLE

1. Two hounds of any sex. A convenient way of counting.
2. A device which assists in controlling or training hounds by keeping two hounds attached to each other.
3. To couple—to attach two hounds together with "couples".

COVERT

(Pronounced "cover"). Woods or brush where fox may be found.

CROP

The stiff part of the hunting whip to which the thong and lash are attached.

CRY

The sound hounds make when hunting.

CUB

A young fox.

CUBHUNTING

Hunting before the formal season starts. Hounds are usually kept in covert and not permitted to chase any fox that goes away. Teaches young hounds and helps to get young cubs in the habit of running straight.

DOUBLE

A series of short sharp notes blown on the horn—"doubling the horn." Signifies fox is afoot.

DOUBLE BACK

If a fox returns to the covert after having once left it it "doubles back".

DRAW

1. "To draw a covert"—to search for a fox in a particular patch of wood, brush, etc.

2. "Draw" is also used as a noun to replace the word "covert" —"Long Copse is a difficult draw."

3. To "draw" a hound, or a group of hounds, is to separate them from the others, in kennels, for a particular purpose.

DRIVE
The desire on the part of a hound to get well forward with the line.

DWELL
To lack drive—to fail to get well forward when hunting.

EARTH
Anywhere a fox goes to ground, but usually a hole where foxes live regularly.

ENTER
To "enter" a hound is to start to use him regularly for hunting.

FEATHER
When a hound waves his stern and indicates by more concentrated activity that he is on a line or near it he is said to "feather".

FIELD
The followers of the hunt, other than the M.F.H. and Staff.

FIELD MASTER
The M.F.H. designates a person to control the field—this is the Field Master.

FIXTURE
A fixture card is sent to all members of the hunt listing the time and place of the meets for a given period.

GROUND
When a fox takes shelter, usually underground, he is said to "go to ground".

HEAD
To cause the fox to turn from his planned direction of travel is "to head the fox".

HEEL
Backwards. When hounds hunt the line in the wrong direction they "hunt the heel line" (also called "counter").

HOLD HARD
"Stop please".

HONOUR
When a hound gives tongue on a line already being hunted by another hound he "honours".

HUNTING WHIP
The crop, thong and lash carried when hunting is correctly known as a "hunting whip" and not a "hunting crop".

HUNTSMAN
The man responsible for controlling hounds in the field is the "huntsman".

LARK
Jumping fences when hounds are not running. Annoys land-owners.

LASH
Short piece of cord attached to the thong of the hunting whip. Sometimes the thong and lash are improperly referred to as a unit and called "lash".

LIFT
When hounds are hunting the huntsman may sometimes carry hounds forward on the line. Known as "lifting" hounds. Risky, should not be done often.

LINE
The trail of the fox.

LITTER
A collection of young born at the same time to the same mother. In hunting generally applied to whelps (puppies) or cubs.

MARK
(Mark the ground). A hound, having stopped at an earth, indi-cates by trying to dig his way in and by giving tongue in a very distinctive way, that a fox has gone to ground.

MASTER OR M.F.H.
Person in command of the Hunt, both in kennels and in the field.

MEET

The assembly of the members of the hunt and the hounds at the start of a day's sport, e.g., "Where is the meet tomorrow?"

NOSE

A hound's ability to detect and interpret the scent is referred to as his "nose".

OPEN

When a hound first gives tongue on a line he is said to "open".

PAD

1. The foot of a fox.
2. The centre cushion of a hound's foot.

POINT

1. The shortest distance between the place where a run began and the place where it ended, e.g., "That was a four mile point, but hounds ran at least eight miles".
2. The position to which the huntsman sends the Whipper-in to watch for a fox to go away.

RATCATCHER

Informal riding clothes (tweed jacket). Correct wear for cubbing.

RATE

To correct hounds with a warning cry. Tone of voice more important than actual words, e.g., "Ware Riot".

RIDE

A cleared path or lane through woods.

RIOT

Rabbit, hare deer, or anything else that hounds should not hunt but might.

RUN

The period of time when hounds are actually hunting on the line of a fox. Usually implies a gallop for the field.

SCENT

A fox's smell. Scent may be good, easy to follow, or bad, difficult to follow, depending partially on the weather.

SPEAK

To give tongue, when referring to a single hound. e.g., "Valiant opened and spoke for some time before the others joined him."

STAFF

Those employed by the hunt—the Huntsman and Whippers-in.

STERN
Hound's tail.

THONG
The long, flexible, plaited leather portion of the hunting whip which is attached to the crop at one end and the lash at the other.

TONGUE
A hound's cry. He "gives tongue" when he is on the line of a fox.

VIEW
To "view" the fox is to catch sight of him.

VIEW HOLLOA
The shout or cry given by a member of the hunt staff on viewing a fox.

WALK
Hound puppies are sent, preferably in couples, to farms and private houses during the summer of their first year. They learn about farm animals, traffic, etc., and are said to be "out to walk".

WARE
Corruption of "beware". Usually pronounced "war".

A warning used (a) to riders, e.g., "Ware wire"; (b) to hounds, e.g., "Ware riot".

WHELP
To whelp—to bear puppies.

A whelp—a hound puppy. "That hound was whelped on such and such a date".

WHIPPER-IN
A member of the hunt staff who helps the Huntsman in the control of hounds.

The Manual of Horsemanship, B.H.S.

Veterinary Notes for Horse Owners, Hayes.

Riding to Hounds in America, William P. Wadsworth, M.F.H., pp. 41-46.

BIBLIOGRAPHY

Veterinary Notes for Horse Owners, by Capt. M. Horace Hayes, F.R.C.V.S. 15th Revised Edition 1964. Revised by J. F. Donald Tutt, F.R.C.V.S. Published by RRCO Publishing Company Inc., New York. Fourth printing 1969.

Practical Farriery, a Guide for Apprentices and Junior Craftsmen, by C. Richardson, F.W.C.F. Published by Sir Isaac Pitman and Sons Ltd., London. First Edition. Reprinted 1965.

First Aid Hints for the Horse Owner. A Veterinary Notebook, by Lt.-Col. W. E. Lyon. Published by Collins, London. Third Edition 1961.

Horseman's Veterinary Adviser, by Joseph B. Davidson, D.V.M. Published by Horse Publications, Columbus, Ohio. First Edition 1966.

The Manual of Horsemanship of the British Horse Society.

Your Horse, A Veterinary Book. Published by Sporting Life Publications.

Top Form Book of Horse Care, by Frederick Harper, Popular Library Edition. Printed in the U.S.A. 1966.

The Design and Construction of Stables and Ancillary Buildings, by Peter C. Smith, A.R.I.B.A. Published by J. A. Allen and Co. Ltd., London. First Edition 1967.

Horses in Action, by R. H. Smythe, M.R.C.V.S. Published by Country Life Ltd., London. Second Impression 1964.

Training the Racehorse, by Lt.-Col. P. D. Stewart, D.S.O. Published by Stanley Paul, London. 2nd Edition, 3rd Impression 1964.

Horse Breeding and Stud Management, by Henry Wynmalen, M.F.H. Published by Country Life Ltd., London. Fourth Impression 1962.

Riding to Hounds in America, an introduction for Foxhunters, by William P. Wadsworth, M.F.H. Published by The Chronicle of the Horse. Third printing 1967.

Saddlery, by E. Hartley Edwards. Published by A. S. Barnes and Co. Inc., New Jersey. Second Printing 1963.

Summerhay's Encylcopædia for Horsemen, compiled by R. S. Summerhays. Published by Frederick Warne and Co. Ltd., London and New York. Fifth Revised Edition 1970.

Stitch by Stitch, by Diana Tuke. Published by J. A. Allen and Co. Ltd., London, 1970.

Bit by Bit, by Diana Tuke. Published by J. A. Allen and Co. Ltd., London, 1965. Reprinted 1969.

INDEX

Rugs and Rollers (blankets), 80, 81
Roughing off, 110

Saddle blanket, 66
Saddle fitting, 63
Saddle sores, 67
Safety stirrups, 57
Sand, 27
Sandcrack, 146
Sawdust, 20, 23, 24, 25
Scalded back, 67
Scapula, 63
Securing horses, 21
Seedy toe, 140
Sesamoiditis, 164
Shavings, 20, 23, 25
Shoeing, 120
Shoulders, 63
Shoulder blades, 65
Sidebone, 134
Site of buildings, 7
Singeing, 83
Sole, 120
    wounds of, 136
Sore back, 65, 171
Sore shins, 164
Soundness of wind, 95
Spavins,
    bone, 152
    bog, 161, 200
Speedy-cut, 134, 148
Spine, 64
Splints, 151
Split hoof, 147
Sprains, 157
Stable rubber, 29, 33
Stable vices, 178
Stall, 15
Stamping and pawing, 89
Strangles, 189
Strapping, 34
Straw, 20
Sugar beet pulp, 45
Suspensory ligament, 158
Sweat scraper, 29
Sweet Itch, 181

Tack, 49
    cleaning, 52
Tail, 84

Teeth, 115
    molars, 177
    sharp, 177
Temperature of stable, 11
Temperature of horse, 95
Tendons, 123
    injury to, 157
Tetanus, 191
Thoroughpin, 162
Throat lash, 58
Thrush, 138
Ticks, 181
Tools, stable, 20
Tourniquet, 169
Tracheotomy, 196
Trailer—see also Horsebox and
    loading, 102
Tushes, 115
Twisted gut—see Colic, 193
"Tying up" (see Azoturia), 190

Undercutting, 134, 149
Urticaria (see Nettlerash), 184

Ventilation, 10, 11, 12
Ventilating Cowls, 12
Ventricle stripping, 196
Vices, stable, 89, et seq.

Walls, 8
Wall of hoof, 120
Warbles, 173
Warmth, 98
Water brush, 29
Water supply, 17, 35, 98
Weaving, 90
Wheat, 44
Whip worms, 175
Whistling, 195
White line (of foot), 122
Window, 12
Wind galls, 163, 202
Wind sucking, 90
Wisp, 29
Withers, 63
Wither pad, 55
Wolf teeth, 73, 115
Worms, worming, 173
    (see also Internal Parasites)
Wounds, 169